Prefaces to Shakespeare

*Coriolanus*

PREFACES TO SHAKESPEARE
by Harley Granville-Barker

The complete Prefaces are available in paperback format, divided into seven volumes:

# Prefaces to
# SHAKESPEARE

Harley Granville-Barker

## *Coriolanus*

B. T. BATSFORD LTD
LONDON

FIRST PUBLISHED 1930
FIRST PUBLISHED IN THIS EDITION 1982

PRINTED IN GREAT BRITAIN
BY BILLING AND SONS LTD, GUILDFORD, LONDON AND WORCESTER
FOR THE PUBLISHERS
**B. T. BATSFORD LTD**
4 FITZHARDINGE STREET, LONDON W1H OAH

ISBN 0 7134 4328 6

# FOREWORD
## by Sir John Gielgud

A NUMBER of older players used to describe Harley Granville-Barker to me very vividly as he was when they had worked with him before the 1914–18 War.

He had been slim and poetic-looking in those days, a vegetarian like his close friend and mentor Bernard Shaw. Wearing sandals and chewing nuts, infinitely demanding as he was when directing Shakespeare, they strove to please him in his striving for perfection, and were lost in admiration of his innovations—an almost uncut text, only two intervals and a simple stylized decor, with a builtout forestage, no footlights, and a breakneck speed in delivery from his cast. On first nights he would pin last minute notes of exhortation on their dressing-room mirrors: 'Be swift, be swift, be not poetical' (to Cathleen Nesbitt as Perdita).

When I first caught sight of him myself in 1928 he looked impressive enough, but more like a successful businessman. He was beginning to put on weight, and wore a dark suit and a Homburg hat. But I was instantly to become aware of his sureness and authority. Even though his wife (watching jealously from the darkness of the dress circle), interrupted him once or twice with a firm 'Harley! lunch . . .' to which, alas, he obediently complied, he had contrived in two short hours to redirect (and even in one of the plays recast the leading part) with unerring and unimpeachable finality.

Though he lived for a time in England, he soon became dissatisfied with trying to become a country squire and moved to Paris. Here he wrote the Shakespeare *Prefaces* and lectured at the Sorbonne. In 1937–8, when he came to see some Shakespearean productions of mine, he wrote me a number of brilliant letters of criticism which I had the good sense to keep. And in 1939, when I was to take *Hamlet* to Elsinore, after a preliminary week at the Lyceum, I heard he was in London and wrote begging him to come to a late rehearsal. Next morning he summoned me to the Ritz, and gave me three hours of invaluable and detailed notes with which I was able to improve my own performance and that of my company.

Finally, in 1940, Lewis Casson and Tyrone Guthrie prevailed on him to help us in a production of *King Lear* at the Old Vic. He stayed at the Athenaeum and for ten days we had him to ourselves. Of those ten days of rehearsals at the Vic I have written some account elsewhere. Even the Fall of France, which was to appal us some weeks later, could not make me forget the magic excitement of working under Barker for those few short days—the agonising struggles to satisfy his demands, the devastating accuracy of his strictures, the enormous satisfaction of earning an occasional note of approval. Then, just after the first dress rehearsal, he was gone, though during the subsequent weeks he would still write me post-cards mentioning points which he had reconsidered and things that he had meant to say.

In 1945 I was playing Hamlet again for the last time and heard he had been to see a matinée. Rather timidly I invited him and his wife to dine with me at my house on the very night when Peace was to be declared. But I found him considerably aged and silent and did not press him to talk about the theatre before his wife. After dinner, however, he did draw me aside and said some kind things about my performance. A few days later he wrote me a last letter, apologising for not having remembered the 1939 production and the help he had given me in improving it.

The following year he died in Paris, but though with a few of his staunchest admirers, I begged to be allowed to organise a Memorial Service, Mrs Barker sent strict injunctions that she had no wish for him to be publicly commemorated 'by actors' and we were forced to abandon the idea. I can hardly believe that Barker would have approved her decision. Though he plainly despised the commercial trappings of our profession—its gossip, intrigue and jealousy, its publicity, cheapness and ephemeral glories and disasters—I cannot but think of him as a great master, the nearest theatrical equivalent to Toscanini among the many brilliant colleagues I have been fortunate to work with during my long career.

July 1981

John Gielgud

# Coriolanus

CORIOLANUS cannot be ranked with the greatest of the tragedies. It lacks their transcendent vitality and metaphysical power. But while neither story nor characters evoke such qualities, those they do evoke are here in full measure. The play is notable for its craftsmanship. It is the work of a man who knows what the effect of each stroke will be, and wastes not one of them. And while ease and simplicity may sometimes be lacking, an uncertain or superfluous speech it would be hard to find. Was Shakespeare perhaps aware of some ebbing of his imaginative vitality—well there may have been after the creation in about as many years of *Othello, King Lear, Antony and Cleopatra* and *Macbeth*! and did he purposefully choose a subject and characters which he could make the most of by judgment and skill?

The play follows close, it would seem, upon *Antony and Cleopatra*. Between the two there is the general likeness of a setting in Roman history. For the rest, the contrasts are so many and so marked as hardly to be fortuitous. To that large picture of an imperial Rome and a decadent Egypt and of

> The triple pillar of the world transformed
> Into a strumpet's fool.

succeeds this story of earlier and austerer days, of a Rome still challengeable by her neighbors, and of a very different hero. Antony and Caius Marcius are men of action both. But Antony is the astute politician too, and by that talent could save himself from disaster if he would—does save himself and has the game in his hands, only to throw it away because

The beds i' the East are soft.

Antony—and Othello and Macbeth too—are soldiers, famous generals; but that is not the side of them we come to know. Coriolanus is the man of action seen in action, and among the heroes of the maturer canon unique in this.[1] He is the younger man, a fighter and a brilliant one, but effectively no more. He is at heart—and despite his trials remains to the end—the incorrigible boy, with "Boy!" for the final insult flung at him by Aufidius that he will at no price swallow. And save in physical valor (of which in the elder, by the plan of the action, we hear but see nothing) in every trait he and Antony radically differ. To the one his men are "my good fellows." He jokes with them, praises them impulsively and generously for their pluck. The other is curt, even to friends and equals, self-conscious, and incapable of the least appeal to the populace he despises. In his contempt for spoils and rewards, in his stubbornness, his aristocratic pride, in his chastity—Virgilia greeting him on his minatory return, it is

> Now, by the jealous queen of heaven, that kiss
> I carried from thee, dear; and my true lip
> Hath virgined it ever since.

—in every significant feature the two stand contrasted.

Then in Cleopatra's place we have Volumnia; for the exotic mistress the Roman mother. Yet each in her fashion brings ruin, to lover or son. And for the Egyptian Court, in which, says Enobarbus,

> Mine and most of our fortunes to-night shall be—drunk to bed.

we exchange that picture of the simple Roman home, its great ladies content to

> *set themselves down on two low stools and sew.*

The contrasts are pervasive too. In the one play the action is spacious and varied beyond comparison; Shakespeare's every resource is drawn upon, his invention finds full scope. In *Coriolanus* it is disciplined, kept to its single channel, and the story moves lucidly and directly to its retributive end. And in one

---

[1] And even Henry V, at war, is not seen fighting. He is the didactic hero, and this is far less mature dramatic work.

major difference most of the rest are rooted: in the part played in each by the idea of Rome. In each, of course, it is a vital part. Antony early forecasts his own ruin in that reckless

> Let Rome in Tiber melt, and the wide arch
> Of the ranged empire fall!

Cleopatra's first note of alarm lest she lose him sounds in the

> He was disposed to mirth; but on the sudden
> A Roman thought hath struck him.

and throughout she is a prey to her jealousy, hatred and dread of Rome. Still, this is little more than a background for the personal passion. But in *Coriolanus* everything centers upon Rome. It is the play's one sounding board. The springs of the action are there. Coriolanus himself sinks at last by comparison to something like second place. He returns for his revenge, and all thoughts and eyes are on him. He departs, self-defeated; and it is Volumnia who re-enters the city in triumph, hailed by a

> Behold our patroness, the life of Rome!

And his death thereafter in Corioles even approaches anticlimax.

But this fidelity to the larger, less personal theme lends the play a very Roman strength and solidity, which compensates to some degree, and in its kind, for the lack of such plenary inspiration as has given us Lear or Macbeth, colossal and then stripped to the soul. The play gains strength too from the keying of its action throughout to strife of one sort or another. Of no other of the plays can it be said that, but for an incidental scene or so, and for the stilled suspense in which we listen to Volumnia's ultimate pleadings, the quarreling and fighting scarcely cease from beginning to end. It is dramatically the more important, then, that the opposing stresses should be kept fairly balanced, in sympathy as well as in force. Amid mere ebb and flow of violence the interest of the action could not be sustained. But the balance is adjusted and continually readjusted, the tension never quite relaxed. And the skill of the play's workmanship shows largely in this.

The story allows for scene after scene of actual fighting, and Shakespeare contrives for these every sort of variety: ranging in the war with the Volscians from the amazing sight of Marcius pitted against a whole city-full to the duel with Aufidius; in the struggle with the citizens from the victory where, sword in hand, he leads a handful of his friends against the rabble, a victory he is persuaded not to pursue, to the defeat in which this same rabble, better disciplined by the Tribunes, combine to banish him. And in the play's closing passages, the happy shouts of the Romans, freed from their fears, are contrasted with the spurious triumph of the Volscians.

The balance of sympathy also is fairly adjusted, neither side capturing—and keeping—overmuch. Shakespeare has been freely charged, in an age apt to be prejudiced in its favor, with bias against the populace. Allow for a little harmless ridicule and it is really not so. They are no match for Menenius in a contest of wit— although one of them, to his surprise, gamely stands up to him— but they see through Marcius' mockery, for all that they are too polite to tell him so. In that scene of the "garment of humility," indeed, his manners contrast most unfavorably with theirs. Individually, they seem simple, kindly creatures; collectively, they are doubtless unwise and unstable. They are human. Marcius has been their enemy, and they do not forget it. He declares that he remains so, and when he attacks them, they retaliate. They follow their leaders blindly, are misled and turn on them savagely at last. It is not a very sentimental survey, certainly. But why should it be?

The Tribunes are left the unqualified "villains of the piece"; a surface of comic coloring—which by making them amusingly contemptible may make them a little less detestable—is the only mitigation allowed them. But not one of the characters with a capital share in the melee of the action is very sympathetically drawn. Not, certainly,

Worthy Menenius Agrippa; one that hath always loved the people.

—so acclaimed by them at our first sight of him, but in fact, as we soon find, cajoling them and sneering at them by turns. Not Aufidius, unstable in good and ill. The untender Volumnia remains so to the last, heedless in her triumph of the price her son must pay for it; a point made implicitly only, but clearly enough to leave us feeling cold towards her. And Shakespeare treats Caius Marcius himself detachedly, as a judge might, without creative warmth. Both sides of his case are to be heard; and we see him first at his worst (an unusual introduction for a titular hero), bullying the hungry citizens. The balance is soon adjusted by evidence—the fighter seen actually fighting—that his valor exceeds all tales of it; in battle and after it he stands out as hero supreme. And his trial of character, when this begins, is lifted, at its crisis, to high ground. It is not his ill-conditioned egoism but his fervent championship of an unpopular faith that gets him driven from Rome. The balance shifts violently when he seeks recreant revenge for this, to be shifted again, when at the last moment he abandons it and pays the penalty. Finally, something like justice is done.

The play's range of characters is not a wide one, for it is kept closely relevant to the demands of the action, and these do not by much overspread the direct channel of the story. But within this range Shakespeare works with complete surety. We have that most leisurely of openings, the tale of the Belly and the Members, and Marcius' first attack on the citizens—much of a distractingly different sort having to happen before that full quarrel is joined—is given good scope. The geography of the battle-scenes by Corioles is schemed for us as concisely as clearly. But we have their action at length; for this serves to fill out the characters of Marcius, of Cominius and Titus Lartius too, each the more himself by contrast with the others; the prudent Consul and the old warrior, so young at heart, who will

> lean upon one crutch and fight with t'other,
> Ere stay behind this business.

generously happy, both of them, in their arrogant young hero's glory. The dispute that leads to the banishment is thrashed out at fullest length, argued back and forth, and yet again, nothing significant left uncanvassed. Later, in the scene at Antium, which brings us the renegade Coriolanus, we note that Shakespeare gives as much space to the sly, flunkey commentings of Aufidius' servants upon the amazing business and their master's romantic aberration as he has to the encounter itself. This, besides lowering the tension, helps resolve the new combination into the unheroic key in which it will be worked out.

Shakespeare has now come to ask for more sheer acting from his actors than he did, for more meaning and feeling to be compressed occasionally into half a dozen words than would once have flowed from a rhetorical hundred, for expressive listening as well as expressive speech, for silence itself sometimes to be made eloquent.

*Holds her by the hand, silent.*

—the play's most tragic moment, in which Marcius accepts defeat and in the sequel death at his mother's hand, confided to a simple stage direction.[2] Throughout the play action and words are expressively keyed together, the action of as great an import as the words. Marcius' share in the scene of the wearing of the gown of humility is as much picturing as speaking; and the mere sight of him later in his Roman dress, surrounded by the Volsces in theirs, sitting in council with them, marching into Corioles at their head—the graphic discord vivifies the play's ending.[3] The sight of the silently approaching figures of Volumnia, Virgilia and Valeria makes double effect; directly upon us, and upon us again through the effect made upon Marcius. And little though Virgilia says (and Valeria not a word), Volumnia so insistently joins them to her plea that their simple presence has an all but articulate value; while the actual spectacle of Marcius fighting singlehanded "within Corioles gates" is better witness to his prowess than any of the "acclamations hyperbolical" which he somewhat self-consciously decries. The memory of it, moreover, will not fade, only lie dormant until at the last it is rekindled by the magnificently trenchant

---

[2] And it is pretty certainly Shakespeare's own. Such moments of eloquent silence are to be found indicated, more or less explicitly, in all the later plays. A very notable one comes with Macbeth's hearing of his wife's death. Another follows upon the blow that Othello publicly deals Desdemona.

[3] In *Cymbeline*, certainly, costume marks the difference between Roman and British, and in *Macbeth* between Scots and English; in *Antony and Cleopatra*, probably, between Roman and Egyptian. We may take for granted, I think, that Volscians and Romans were dressed distinctively. A "realistic" reading may suggest that Marcius would cast off his Roman garb with his allegiance. But I believe that, quitting the "mean apparel" in which he went to encounter Aufidius, he would reappear as a Roman general, the dramatic effect being worth more than any logic.

"Boy"! false hound!
If you have writ your annals true, 'tis there,
That, like an eagle in a dove-cote, I
Fluttered your Volscians in Corioles:
Alone I did it.

Here, then, we have a play of action dealing with men of action; and in none that Shakespeare wrote do action and character better supplement and balance each other.

## The Characters

### CAIUS MARCIUS

MARCIUS is by no means a sympathetic character, and Shakespeare's attitude towards him seems, as we say, to be less that of a creator than a judge. There is a sense in which—brought to it by the art of dramatist and actor—we can come to "sympathize" even with the murderer Macbeth, as we can pity the murderer Othello, having learned to put ourselves imaginatively in their place. But we are left detached observers of Coriolanus; now admiring his valor, now exasperated by his harsh folly, touched occasionally by the flashes of nobility, the moments of gentleness. Yet we are never wholly at one with him, never made free of the inward man. And the juncture which could best bring this into play, the spiritual crisis in which he decides for his renegade revenge on Rome, is boldly and neatly side-stepped. It is strange, says Marcius in that one short soliloquy, how quickly enemies may become friends and friends turn enemies.

So with me:
My birth-place hate I, and my love's upon
This enemy town.

We are (this is to tell us) past the play's turning point already. The crucial change in the man has already taken place; and of the process of it we learn nothing. But this is not necessarily a shortcoming on Shakespeare's part—as were Marcius a Hamlet it would be. *Was* there any such explicable process? He is not a man of reason, but of convictions and passionate impulses, which can land him in a sudden decision—and he will not know how he came by it. That may help make him a good fighter, less good,

probably, as a general, certainly a poor politician. And it justifies
Shakespeare's treatment of him here. By his mere looks, in the
bitter humility—the old pride so quickly breaking through, as the
unlucky Third Servingman discovers—with which he encourages
Aufidius' servants to mock him, we are to discern the sufferings
of his lonely exile, and surmise the pent-up wrath, vented at last
in that blind resolve to be revenged on his own ungrateful
people or let the Volsces take revenge on him. Shall we now, on
such evidence, sufficiently surmise all this? That the thing, when
it did happen, will have happened in a flash; we have seen amply
enough of him by now to believe so. Critics have combed the text
for some sign of the actual moment of its happening; since
surely, they argue, Shakespeare could not have let such a
significant one slip by unmarked; and one has been found hidden
in an exclamatory "O, the gods!" wrung from him at the very
time of his banishing when he is taking leave of his mother and
his wife. But this will not do. Tell the actor concerned that he
is expected to convey to his audience in those three detached and
unacknowledged words a sudden resolve to be revenged on the
ungrateful city, and he will reasonably reply that it cannot be
done. And while the maturer Shakespeare may certainly present
his actors now and then with all but insuperable difficulties—
creative imagination beckoning the interpreter towards very steep
places indeed—never does he ask of them the impossible. What
he does in this instance by a mere stroke of omission may seem to
the *reader* of the play only to leave a rent in the texture of story
and character. But in effect, and to the *spectator*, it is not so.
Marcius could not appropriately be made to argue himself into
such treason, as a Hamlet might, or discover the seeds of it in
his nature, as might Macbeth. But picture and action significantly
"placed" are as legitimate and often as important a dramatic
resource as the spoken word can be. And what, at this juncture,
could be more fittingly eloquent than the simple sight—and the
shock it must give us—of this haggard, hardly recognizable
figure? It will flash into our imaginations, as words might not,
a sense of the suffering that has brought him to such a pass.

Shakespeare does not shirk the less tolerable aspects of the
character. Indeed he stresses them, since he first shows us the man
at his worst—strange treatment for a hero!—and in the theater

first impressions cut deep. After the long and exceptionally leisurely opening of the tale of the Belly and the Members comes Marcius, like a tornado, bullying and abusing the hungry citizens; and while what he says of them may be true, it is no satisfying answer to their empty stomachs. But if this is the worst side of him the best side of that is turned to us a minute later, and within a few more the various contending forces of this most contentious of plays have been deployed, their differences established, Marcius in the center of them.

Word comes that the Volsces are in arms, threatening Rome. He turns happily to welcome the news, and the war itself, which he has shrewdly foreseen. It will help "vent our musty superfluity"; here is something quite other than the complaint that has driven the despised citizens (who listen in glum silence) to mutiny. To "our best elders," the Consul Cominius and the Senators, who now appear, he is all disciplined deference, accepting, though, besides, their tributes paid to him as if these were his right, nor forgetting as he goes to fling a parting sneer at the "worshipful mutiners."

The new-made Tribunes, Brutus and Sicinius, have been listening in silence too; and now we have their comments on him, as unfriendly, truly, as his own conduct to the people they are to stand for has been unfair—unfair to the best in his nature, but an undeniable part of that truth about him which the play is so judicially to unfold. Proud, disdainful, insolent; the three notes are hit hard. The Tribunes attach to him by implication besides—as such men are apt to—some of their own politician's cunning. But in this, it will soon be made plain, they mistake him. Better for him had he had that sort of weapon with which to fight them.

The battle-scenes bring his most trenchant qualities into play. The amazing spectacle of his singlehanded fight "within Corioles gates" is to be matched by his duel with Aufidius in which he takes on "certain Volsces" too who come to their leader's aid, *till they be driven in breathless,* later by his stand against his fellow Romans, drawing his sword with a "No; I'll die here," and contrasted with the yet later sight of him, truly alone, *in mean apparel, disguised and muffled.* Throughout the battle he is in his glory, and at his happiest, outshining and outtopping all the rest; hero indeed. But the more portraying strokes are not

neglected. When his troops fall back he abuses them as roundly
as he did the citizens; still this is in the stress of the fighting.
When he calls inspiringly for volunteers to follow him in a
desperate venture—

> If any such be here,
> As it were sin to doubt, that love this painting
> Wherein you see me smeared; if any fear
> Lesser his person than an ill report;
> If any think brave death outweighs bad life,
> And that his country's dearer than himself . . .

—these surly cowards of such a short while since, now *all shout
and wave their swords; take him up in their arms, and cast up
their caps.*[4] Marcius could win men if he would, it is plain, had
he but a tithe of the confidence in them that he has in himself.
Nor is it that he is mere cold-hearted egoist. At the very instant
of victory he can remember the "poor man," a prisoner, who once
used him kindly, even as later, in the midst of his triumph he
can think of the widows left in Corioles and the "mothers that
lack sons." He shows contempt for the spoils of war, honest
distaste for the praises his prowess wins him, and under their
lavishing an all but boyish self-consciousness.

This last trait (of Shakespeare's own importing: it has no
place in Plutarch) is turned to varying account throughout the
play. In the boyishness, the reckless high spirits with which he
flings himself into battle, there is saving grace; even the thrasoni-
cal bragging to Aufidius before they fight is purged of offense if
it comes as their mere overflow.[5] The question is not one of
years. Marcius' actual age is not determined, and in North is
only implied by the fact that he first went to the wars "being but
a strippling," and that when he stands for Consul he has seen
seventeen years' service. He might then, by this, be about thirty-
two, and as mature a man as the maturer Hamlet. But more than
one thing in the story gives color to youthfulness of temper. His

---

[4] It was not, truly, this division of the army which fled and left him to his
fate "within Corioles gates." But while we shall remark the contrast in spirit
and conduct, we shall not, I think—and are not meant to—make the nicer
distinction.

[5] Note, too, that there is something of the duelists' conventional salute in this,
as it might be a clashing of sword against shield.

boyish prowess, repeatedly stressed, suggests it; so do his rash
decisions; so does his continued deference to his mother. And
Shakespeare takes and enlarges on this means of mitigating the
harshness which makes him—as North has it—so "churlish,
uncivill and altogether unfit for any man's conversation," to touch
him with an unruly charm instead.

It is in the self-consciousness that the flaw lies. His repeated
protests against the praises lavished on him become somewhat less
then genuine. During the traffic of the battle, to generous old
Titus Lartius:

> Sir, praise me not;
> My work hath yet not warmed me. . . .

And again:

> Pray now, no more: my mother,
> Who has a charter to extol her blood,
> When she does praise me, grieves me. . . .

And yet again, in protest to his general, not very graciously:

> You shout me forth
> In acclamations hyperbolical;
> As if I loved my little should be dieted
> In praises sauced with lies.

—this is not modesty (as Cominius kindly calls it), rather an
inverted pride. Neglect to praise him; he will be the first to
resent that!

We are shown one aspect after another of this obsessing self-
consciousness. He will not even make himself sit still and listen
respectfully to the Senate's official tribute to him, but must be up
and away in the middle of it with a

> I had rather have one scratch my head i' the sun
> When the alarum were struck than idly sit
> To hear my nothings monstered.

His desperate discomfort standing in the market place in the
gown of humility is positively comic.

> May I change these garments?

—his first request when the ordeal is over. He pictures himself
with dramatic clarity returning there shamefaced to ask pardon

of the despised citizens; he cannot resist, even at this critical moment, the false modesty of

> Scratches with briers;
> Scars to move laughter only.

when his friends once more be-laud his "war-like service" and cite his many wounds. Later, he is most conscious of the effect he is making in his picturesque disgrace upon Aufidius and the lackeys. Lastly, he provokes his own death by losing all control under the petty insult of Aufidius' "Boy!"

Yet such self-consciousness is not self-knowledge. Possessing but a spice of *this*, would he ever have taken his rash, revengeful vow to destroy Rome?—which, put to the ultimate test, proves no more stable than does Aufidius' febrile conversion to his cause. At the critical moment he stands firm against Cominius, certainly. But with Menenius—though he dismissed him harshly— he has afterwards to own that, under guise of firmness, he *has* yielded, even if it be only "a very little." And the mere news of the coming of his wife and mother seems to paralyze him:

> Shall I be tempted to infringe my vow
> In the same time 'tis made? I will not.

—the desperate "I will not" telling us plainly that in his heart he knows already that he will. He is no true renegade. Striving to be false to Rome, he is false to himself. And this his instinct—his unclouded, unself-conscious self-knowledge—has warned him more than once that he cannot afford to be. He was so—if harmlessly; for it was a trivial matter, and Shakespeare stresses the comic aspect of it—when after swearing he never would he *did* put on the gown of humility. He is about to be again, and in a matter of more consequence, when, under protest—

> Would you have me
> False to my nature? Rather say I play
> The man I am.

—he is letting Volumnia persuade him to recant before the people the faith he has just so ardently professed to them. But he finds when he tries to that he cannot. And it is in the violent recoil from this attempt to be other than he is that he strikes his most

genuinely heroic note, with the ineffably proud retort to his
sentence of banishment, the "I banish you."

Wrong-headed, intolerant and intolerable in his dealings with
the citizens he may be, but upon the actual issues between them
is he so wrong? He foresaw the first Volscian attack when the
Senators—"our best elders"—did not, and the hungry populace
could think of nothing but their hunger. Victory won and a
"good" peace granted the enemy (a little to his impatience),
himself made Consul, he foresees another attack—

> So then the Volsces stand but as at first,
> Ready, when time shall prompt them, to make road
> Upon's again.

—not imagining, however, who, in the amazing irony of events,
will lead it! He has foreseen, besides, from the beginning, that
the new-made Tribunate

> will in time
> Win upon power, and throw forth greater themes
> For insurrections arguing.

And who is to say that he is wrong in his protest against the
"popular shall . . . the greater poll . . . the yea and no of general
ignorance" being let outweigh experienced wisdom. What answer
is there to his passionate

> my soul aches
> To know, when two authorities are up,
> Neither supreme, how soon confusion
> May enter, 'twixt the gap of both and take
> The one by the other.

Wrong or right, however, he must abide by his own convictions:
honestly he can no other. He foresaw that too from the beginning,
when Volumnia first held him out hopes of the consulate and he
told her:

> Know, good mother,
> I had rather be their servant in my way
> Than sway with them in theirs.

For a man can do no better than be himself at his best. Sometimes
it may even strangely seem that his quality lies rather in the worse
than the better part of him; then we must take the rough with
the smooth.

Play and character become truly tragic only when Marcius, to be traitor to Rome, must turn traitor to himself. The actual turning, as we said, we do not see, we are shown the thing already inwardly done. And the tragedy is uncovered in something like a reversal of the process, in the tragic failure to undo the thing once done, once begun even. It is ironic tragedy, too. Marcius has been used to meet fortune, good or bad, in the open. But from that dark moment in Antium, of the bitter

> My birth-place hate I, and my love's upon
> This enemy town.

everything with him and within him turns to mockery. Aufidius' extravagant homage to him will soon show itself a cheat. It is a false façade of him seeming to sit there

> in gold, his eye
> Red as 'twould burn Rome . . .

And when he has finally yielded to his mother's prayers he looks up to find that

> the heavens do ope,
> The gods look down, and this unnatural scene
> They laugh at.

He could go back to Rome—the "clusters who did hoot him out o' the city" now as ready to "roar him in again"—thanked for his weakness and kindness, and forgiven—he Coriolanus forgiven! But nor is that his nature. He is at least no weathercock. He has turned aginst the Romans, he will stay loyal now to the Volsces.[6]

Mockery piles on mockery in Corioles. The people there are something the same problem that they were in Rome. Aufidius, with his great repute, has still to observe their temper. And of Coriolanus, even of him, it can be said that he

> Intends to appear before the people, hoping
> To purge himself with words.. . . .

And—though first, truly, to the lords of the city—so, *the Com-*

---

[6] Tennyson finds a similar thought for

> His honour rooted in dishonour stood
> And faith, unfaithful, kept him falsely true.

*moners being with him,* he does, boasting of the spoils and the
full third part
The charges of the action . . .

he has brought back. When till now did he value such pinchbeck
glory? In Rome he was plunged from triumph into obloquy.
Now it is the fickle commoners of Corioles that turn on him,
cheering him back at one moment, tearing him to pieces the next.
When last these same Volsces swarmed round him he was one
against all of them, and victor. They make better business of it
now.

Coriolanus, then, is a character not inwardly evolved, as the
greater tragic characters are, but seen from without. Seen and
molded, however, in the round; and as consistent and solid a
figure as Shakespeare ever put in motion.

## VOLUMNIA

The relations between mother and son and the likeness and
difference between them are at the core of the play. The likeness
is patent. It is she, he is wont to say, whose praise first made him
a soldier. She rejoices in his prowess, gleefully in his very wounds,
has the tale of them by heart, could dance for joy at his return for
the third time with the oaken garland, wounded yet again. If
martial spirit were all she would seem to be almost more soldier
than he. And when the fateful struggle between them comes it is
the grimmer for this.

As a woman she has no overt part in the political quarrel with
the Tribunes; and, in that phase of the action, it is not until, amid
the violence of its crisis, Marcius seeks a breathing-space in his
house and hers, that we see or hear from her at all. But then she
astonishes us—and him. For until now she has seemed as stiff, and
stiffer than he, in pride. As to the Tribunes and their kind, she
has ignored them, but had been wont, he says,

> To call them woollen vessels, things created
> To buy and sell with groats, to show bare heads
> In congregations, to yawn, be still and wonder
> When one but of my ordinance stood up
> To speak of peace or war . . .

Yet now, when trouble comes, from unashamed policy she

would have him humble himself to them, recant his word and cheat them even in recanting, "mountebank their loves." He is to be, he protests, false to his nature; and she is setting him an example by being false to hers. She persuades him to it: yet fruitlessly since, tested, his nature rebels. It will take more than this: defeat and banishment and, later, suffering and blind anger, to trap him into swearing that oath of unnatural vengeance which it will prove beyond his power to keep. She will set out again to persuade him to break it, and, spending her last ounce of strength and influence, she will succeed. And then it will bear fruit; salvation for Rome, but, for him, bitter fruit indeed.

In a central scene, then, and at one of the play's chief turning points, we have this truly unexpected exhibition of difference between the two. Willful and stubborn he may be, but, to his credit, he is not the mere overgrown spoiled child which the extravagance of her praise might so easily have made him. He turns from praise with the touch of affectation we have noted; from hers the more genuinely, remembering how much he once owed to it. But in his quarrel with the Tribunes he stands fearlessly for a cause. This is enshrined in egoism doubtless, but is not, he proudly feels, the poorer for that; since he stands, in what he has done and is, for what is best in Rome and he will never shrink from proclaiming it and his faith in it, no matter the moment's consequence. Volumnia, astonishingly the opposite, shows herself at once shrewdly critical, worldly-wise—

> O, sir, sir, sir,
> I would have had you put your power well on
> Before you had worn it out.

—and shrewder yet:

> You might have been enough the man you are
> With striving less to be so. . . .

with irony to follow for the deflating of his anger, and the cold realism of

> I have a heart as little apt as yours,
> But yet a brain that leads my use of anger
> To better vantage.

—a calculated use of it. And it will no more dishonor him (she

easily argues) to maneuver a crooked way back into his fellow
countrymen's favor than it would in wartime to

> take in a town with gentle words.

She herself, here and now, lavishes the gentlest on him; these
failing, tries her "use of anger," pretended or real, with a

> At thy choice, then:
> To beg of thee it is my more dishonour
> Than thou of them. Come all to ruin. . . .
> Do your will.

*He* is the cause she stands for—that is the truth; and that he
will not help her, and himself, by unscrupulously putting it
before all other, exasperates her. He pays in banishment the
penalty of his scruples. She is passionately for him in defeat as in
victory, and but the more enraged with his enemies for their
profiting by his high-minded unwisdom. After this, again, she is
absent from the action for many scenes; and again, re-entering it,
she sounds an unexpected note.

Mark now the dramatic strategy, as Shakespeare plans it, of
her share in the women's appeal to Marcius for mercy upon Rome.
Simply the sight of her and of his wife and son stirs him. She
does not speak at first; only

> My mother bows,
> As if Olympus to a molehill should
> In supplication nod. . . .

The constricted figure has an eloquence of its own. His wife,
softly reproachful, wins the first response from him. Not until he
kneels does Volumnia speak, outdoing him then by herself
kneeling, a shade of irony—no more!—in the ostentation of her
gesture. After which, as with a certain confidence in this their
meeting again, the plea is launched. She can be eloquent now, as
never before. It is an eloquence inspired by that clarity of vision
which imminent tragedy brings:

> for how can we,
> Alas! how can we for our country pray,
> Whereto we are bound, together with thy victory,
> Whereto we are bound? Alack! or we must lose
> The country, our dear nurse, or else thy person,
> Our comfort in the country. We must find

> An evident calamity, though we had
> Our wish, which side should win; for either thou
> Must, as a foreign recreant, be led
> With manacles through our streets, or else
> Triumphantly tread on thy country's ruin,
> And bear the palm for having bravely shed
> Thy wife and children's blood.

The new note follows; a new note indeed:

> If it were so that our request did tend
> To save the Romans, thereby to destroy
> The Volsces whom you serve, you might condemn us
> As poisonous of your honour: no; our suit
> Is that you reconcile them: while the Volsces
> May say "This mercy we have showed"; the Romans,
> "This we received"; and each in either side
> Give the all-hail to thee, and cry "Be blest
> For making up this peace!"

If he "mused" before at her indifference to his heroic stand against the mob for his proud conscience' sake, what will his retort be now to this talk of peace—of peace for its own sake; to such a warning from her as

> Thou knowest, great son,
> The end of war's uncertain. . . .

to her disparaging

> Thou hast affected the fine strains of honour. . . .

her

> Think'st thou it honourable for a noble man
> Still to remember wrongs?

It has taken truly a terrible revolution to bring her to this: no less than the sight of her son, his country's hero, turned his country's enemy, her own son, her enemy. And she begins to feel nevertheless that she is beaten, that her high arguments are breaking against his stubborn silence. Yet she is as tenacious a fighter in her way as ever we have found him to be, and she flings herself and the forces with her—mother, wife, child, the whole womanhood of Rome—desperately into the struggle:

> Daughter, speak you:
> He cares not for your weeping. Speak thou, boy:

> Perhaps thy childishness will move him more
> Than can our reasons.

Their silence had begun it, as they stood ranged accusingly before him; by some means they must break his silence now. Volumnia chides and clamors:

> There's no man in the world
> More bound to's mother; yet here he lets me prate
> Like one i' the stocks. Thou has never in thy life
> Shewed thy dear mother any courtesy. . . .

By whatever means let her win! But she can fight a losing battle as fiercely as he could a winning one:

> Down, ladies; let us shame him with our knees.

Then with a Parthian scorn:

> Come, let us go:
> This fellow had a Volscian to his mother:
> His wife is in Corioles, and his child
> Like him by chance.

Yet she has won. Throwing her strength in to the very last, even at the admitted moment of defeat—

> Yet give us our despatch:
> I am husht until our city be a-fire,
> And then I'll speak a little.

—she had already won.

The very moment during his tenacious silence when his will yielded has been covered by silence too. And now she does not answer his low, searching

> O, mother, mother!
> What have you done?

when it emerges from the silence, nor respond at all to the unequivocal

> O, my mother, mother! O!
> You have won a happy victory to Rome;
> But for your son, believe it, O, believe it,
> Most dangerously you have with him prevailed,
> If not most mortal to him.

So possessed by her victory, is she, as to be incapable of a second thought? Is she so spent with the strain of her pleading that she faces Rome again a little later, and its frenzied welcome, in a very daze? Marcius, in any case, as with a new-learned magnanimity, shepherds away more talk of his defeat, thoughts of his fate. And her part in the play is done.[7]

It ends, as does her son's—as may be said of the whole play—amid the ironic laughter of the gods; she is unaware, that is all, of the successive mockeries in the event, made at last so bitterly plain to him. She has bred him to be at once Rome's hero and Rome's enemy. She has begged Rome's life of him, and, in

---

[7] What exactly is the effect that Shakespeare means to have made here? The mere suggestion of his danger in Marcius'

O, mother, mother!
What have you done? . . .

Volumnia, not yet certain of her victory, might easily overlook. But the repeated

O, my mother, mother! O!
You have won a happy victory to Rome;
But for your son, believe it, O, believe it,
Most dangerously you have with him prevailed,
If not most mortal to him.

—to ignore this practically plain statement that he is most likely to be going to his death she must be prostrated indeed. And that I think on the whole is the intention. He then turns and goes to Aufidius, and Volumnia, left among the women, quickly recovers. She has not fainted, there must be no such weakness; it is simply a moment's reaction from the extreme strain of the victory. He turns back, and apostrophizes them from where he stands:

O, mother! wife!

and stands still gazing while Aufidius speaks his aside. This is the heartfelt farewell he takes.

Editors hereabouts insert

*The Ladies make signs to Coriolanus.*

presumably to account for the "Ay, by and by . . ." with which he breaks the silence of his gaze. They stand expectantly where he has left them; there is no need of more. Then he joins them, as if bidding them dismiss all forebodings, gallantly congratulating them on their victory; and our query, if there was risk of one: why does not Volumnia see that in saving Rome she has sent her son to his death? has been fended off. It may return on reflection when the play is over. It probably will not. And if it takes the shape of the memory of a Volumnia as peremptory and passionate as her son, as stubborn in her own cause and as oblivious to all besides, that is a not unjust one.

Shakespeare the practical playwright, having had his full use of a character, and the whole action being near its end, will add nothing needlessly. Volumnia has saved Rome, and the action asks no more of her. Care for her son's fate would prolong or complicate it, and, in doing so, upset the balance of interest. It must suffice, then, that we do not remark any such omission; and circumstance and character are shaped so that we shall not. It is in these instances of dramatic tact that Shakespeare the playwright shows at his most skillful.

winning it, is obviously sending him to his death. And we last
see her welcomed triumphantly back to Rome even as he once
was, flowers strewed before her, amid cries of

> Unshout the noise that banished Marcius;
> Repeal him with the welcome of his mother. . . .

But it is too late for that. And tragedy of character does not
work out in such happy confusions of popular acclaim.

It is a chill parting, this with Volumnia; our last sight of her—
nothing nearer—parading through Rome, her back turned upon
Marcius himself and the essential tragedy's imminent consummation.

## AUFIDIUS

It takes all Shakespeare's skill to make Aufidius fully effective
within the space which the planning of the action allows him—
and perhaps he does not wholly succeed. For a while it is not so
difficult. He is admitted on all hands to be Marcius' rival and
to come short of him by little. Marcius' first word of him is that

> I sin in envying his nobility,
> And were I anything but what I am,
> I would wish me only he.

He is secondary hero. And when within a moment or so we see the
man himself he is telling the Senators of Corioles:

> If we and Caius Marcius chance to meet,
> 'Tis sworn between us we shall ever strike
> Till one can do no more.

Volumnia, imagining glorious things, can see her Marcius

> pluck Aufidius down by the hair . . .

In' the battle the Corioles taunt the Romans with

> There is Aufidius: list, what work he makes
> Amongst your cloven army.

while to Marcius, whether far off—

> There is the man of my soul's hate, Aufidius. . . .

—or within reach—

> Set me against Aufidius and his Antiats. . . .

—he is an obsession. And when they do meet and fight, Aufidius, if bettered, is not beaten. To this point, then, however little we may see of him, he is brought to our minds in each succeeding scene, and is emphatically lodged there when he is so unconsentingly rescued in the duel with his famous enemy by "certain Vol ces" (anonymous: common soldiers presumably, therefore):

> Officious, and not valiant, you have shamed me
> In your condemned seconds.

And, since we shall not see him thereafter for some time, this note of shame, and of the crooked passion it can rouse in the man, is enlarged and given what will be memorable place in a scene coming but a little later.

> Five times, Marcius,
> I have fought with thee; so often hast thou beat me,
> And wouldst do so, I think, should we encounter
> As often as we eat.[8]

Frank confession! But now

> mine emulation
> Hath not that honour in't it had; for where
> I thought to crush him in an equal force,
> True sword to sword, I'll potch at him some way
> Or wrath or craft may get him. . . .
> Where I find him, were it
> At home, upon my brother's guard, even there,
> Against the hospitable canon, would I
> Wash my fierce hands in's heart.

We shall certainly recall that—and be given good cause to—when, all amazingly, the event so falls out. The scheme of the action allows Aufidius very limited space; but we have thus far been kept conscious of him throughout. From now, even until he emerges into it again, he does not go quite without mention, and we shall have lodged in mind what he may mean to it when he does. It is able stagecraft.

In a cruder play Aufidius and the Volsces might be made to serve as "villains of the piece." But Shakespeare is not painting in such ultra-patriotic black and white. We are on the Roman

---

[8] Later on, in Antium, Aufidius makes it "Twelve several times" that he has been beaten. But nothing hangs on the precise number, and he is not on his oath.

side, and they are "foreigners"; so their worse, not their better,
aspect is naturally turned towards us. The victorious Romans
give them a "good" peace, Titus Lartius being commanded to
send back from their captured city

> to Rome
> The best, with whom we may articulate,
> For their own good and ours.

They, when their victorious turn comes, so we hear,

> looked
> For no less spoil than glory . . .

Shakespeare shades them somewhat. But the balance is not
unfairly held.

Aufidius, then, re-enters the action at its most critical juncture,
and to play for the moment a surprising part in it. Here, in this
wine-flushed host to the nobles of Antium, is quite another man;
and not only in the look of him but, yet more surprisingly—
suspense resolved—in the deep-sworn enemy turned ecstatic
comrade. From that

> Nor sleep, nor sanctuary,
> Being naked, sick, nor fane nor Capitol,
> The prayers of priests, nor times of sacrifice,
> Embarquements all of fury, shall lift up
> Their rotten privilege and custom 'gainst
> My hate to Marcius.

we are at a glowing

> Let me twine
> Mine arms about that body, where against
> My grained ash an hundred times hath broke
> And scarred the moon with splinters: here I clip
> The anvil of my sword, and do contest
> As hotly and as nobly with thy love
> As ever in ambitious strength I did
> Contend against thy valour.

It is a turning point indeed, and doubly so; the revolution in
Marcius is barely set forth before it is matched with this. The two
revolutions differ as the two men do; the one a plunging
through defeat and misery from confident pride to obdurate
bitterness; that in Aufidius a sudden emotional overthrow,

sprung by this startling proffer, this attack upon a weakness in him which he would never think to defend. Yet there is a likeness between them too. And they are in keeping, both, with the rest of the play, its extremes of passion and their instabilities; the weathercock-swaying of the citizens, Volumnia's violence and arbitrary shifts. Marcius himself we shall see will be unable to abide by his treason to the end; and Aufidius, we shall very quickly guess, will not long sustain this unnatural change. Recurring ironies fitting into the scheme of tragic irony which informs the whole action.

This "strange alteration"—reflected too in the freakish comment of the servants—gives us a fresh, and, for the moment, an alert interest in Aufidius. From now to the end the stagecraft actuating him remains as able; and if here and there the figure seems to lack vitality, to be a little word-locked, why, livelier development of this new aspect of the man might well make more demands on the play's space than could be spared, or such a turn of inspiration as Shakespeare (even he!) has not unquestionably at command. But he does not dodge nor skip a step in the completing of the character. And, within a scene or so, to begin this, we see Aufidius again—quite disillusioned.

Thinking better of things is a dry business; and this ancillary scene, shared with an anonymous Lieutenant, will appropriately be none of the liveliest. But the matter of it is a strengthening rivet in the character scheme of the play. Aufidius' sobered reaction from his rhapsodies to the coldest common sense—hints dropped moreover of revengeful traps already laid for Marcius; Aufidius to be revenged on him for his own access of too generous folly, the hardest thing forgivable—this will redress any balance of sympathy lost between the two for the action's last phase. We have no violent swing back to the fanatically sportsmanlike hatred with which they started. On the contrary, to Aufidius is given in the scene's last speech the most measured and balanced of summarizings of his rival's qualities and failings. And for Marcius it is in this quiet reasonable accounting that his worst danger can be foreseen. Mastery in soldiership—who has ever denied him that? He has not even to exercise it now:

> All places yield to him ere he sits down;
> And . . .

—despite his treason; because of it indeed—

> the nobility of Rome are his:
> The Senators and Patricians love him too. . . .
> I think he'll be to Rome
> As is the asprey to the fish, who takes it
> By sovereignty of nature. . . .

Aufidius, lacking just that sovereignty, could not look his own problem more fairly in the face. For, indeed, he had better know just where he has the worse of it, that being the second-rate man's due approach to getting the better of it after all. He may next encourage himself by listing—though with every scruple and reserve—Marcius' failings too: pride, temper, intolerance and the rest, and by recognizing that in this discordant world men have the defects of their qualities and the qualities of their defects; and that at best, what is more,

> our virtues
> Lie in the interpretation of the time. . . .

—which may prove for us or against us; and whichever way

> One fire drives out one fire; one nail, one nail;
> Rights by rights founder, strengths by strengths do fail.

Fortune, with a little patient aid, is ever ready to turn her wheel:

> When, Caius, Rome is thine
> Thou art poor'st of all; then shortly art thou mine.

Both speech and scene demand of their audience close attention, closer, perhaps, than such detached argument will currently command at this juncture in a play unless it be embodied in some central, radiating figure. It is the more notable that Shakespeare should here, so to speak, be forcing his meaning through the recalcitrant lines.[9] But his aim, it would seem, is to give a rational substance to the figure, of such a sort as will keep us an Aufidius expressively if cryptically observant through succeeding scenes while we await the due restoring of the natural open enmity between the two.

It comes with relief.

> How is it with our general?

---

[9] One or two lines in this last speech are doubtless corrupt. But rectify them as we may, we shall hardly make them lucid.

his fellow conspirators ask.

> Even so
> As with a man by his own alms empoisoned,
> And with his charity slain.

But he is free now of his false position and on his own ground
again, and the ills done him are glib upon his tongue. He must
be cautiously in the right at all points:

> And my pretext to strike at him admits
> A good construction. I raised him, and I pawned
> Mine honour for his truth. . . .

More than so, he

> took some pride
> To do myself this wrong . . .

—he is fueling up with virtuous indignation, until, at the touch
of a match, Coriolanus himself can be trusted to fire out in fury,
no moral excuses needed. "Traitor . . . unholy braggart . . . boy
of tears . . . boy!"—it is the last spark that sets all ablaze.

Aufidius' philosophic mind has not endured; nor does the
one-time gallantry. "My valour's poisoned . . ." —we are back at
that. He is no coward, we know; has ever been ready to fight.
It is only that, now or never, he must have the best of it, and he
has made all sure. So, duly provoked

> *The Conspirators draw, and kill Coriolanus, who falls.* . . .

Upon which, though, he cannot resist it:

> *Aufidius stands on him.*[10]

Shakespeare, in the maturity of his skill, knows how to give
as much meaning to a significantly placed gesture as to a speech
or more. There are two gestures here, the insolent treading of
the slain man under foot, with the quick attempt in face of the
shocked outcry to excuse it:

> My noble masters, hear me speak.

then the response to the reproach:

> O, Tullus!
> Thou hast done a deed whereat valour will weep.
> Tread not upon him. Masters . . .

---

[10] Shakespeare's own stage direction, we may once more be pretty sure.

which can but be its shamed and embarrassed lifting, the more eloquent of Aufidius, this. The more fittingly unheroic, besides, the ending. The lords of the city have been honourable enemies.

> Peace, ho! no outrage: peace!
> The man is noble and his fame folds in
> This orb o' the earth. His last offences to us
> Shall have judicious hearing.

The sight of the outrage done him horrifies them. But as Aufidius promptly argues,

> My lords, when you shall know, as in this rage
> Provoked by him, you cannot, the great danger
> Which this man's life did owe you, you'll rejoice
> That he is thus cut off.

and, truly, as they'll in fairness soon admit:

> His own impatience
> Takes from Aufidius a great part of blame. . . .

Common sense supervenes:

> Let's make the best of it.

And Aufidius can say with truth, the man being safely dead:

> My rage is gone,
> And I am struck with sorrow.

## MENENIUS

Menenius makes one in the ironically figured pattern of character. He is set outwardly—and at the play's very start—in sharp contrast to Coriolanus himself:

> Worthy Menenius Agrippa; one that hath always loved the people.

—so even the disgruntled citizens admit. Jovial, humorous, reasonable; what could be less like the intolerant, rough-tongued young soldier, whose pride it is that

> He would not flatter Neptune for his trident,
> Or Jove for's power to thunder.

But soon enough we notice that behind the cajoling

> Why, masters, my good friends, mine honest neighbours . . .

and the merry tale that sets them laughing—at each other it is, too!—his complete indifference to their troubles. Marcius, storming, would have had

> the nobility lay aside their ruth,
> And let me use my sword.

Menenius has taken the cannier way; and here already, at no cost but fair words,

> these are almost thoroughly persuaded;
> For though abundantly they lack discretion,
> Yet are they passing cowardly

Nor does he scruple, it would seem, to say so in their hearing.

Menenius is to pervade the play, yet as an auxiliary character only. This full and vivid shaping of the figure so early has one incidental advantage then; the lightest future touch—and however slight be its connection with the main action—will be effective. And in all the plays there are few livelier or more individual characters.

An old gentleman of "character," an "original," to his friends the best of friends; his fighting spirit has not flagged either with the years, and he fights the more cleverly with his tongue for his sole weapon, if the more spitefully now and then. Would Marcius but profit by it his counsel might steer him to safety. He loves him as a man his own son, delights in his prowess and fame. He knows him too, better than does Volumnia, and is quick to persuade him that, willy-nilly, he must don that vext "gown of humility," sticks to him too till he has it on, shepherds him to the very verge of the actual ordeal, only quits him then with almost comic misgiving, to return at the first moment as proud as a nurse of a well-behaved child at a party.

The rioting in the market place tells on his age. While he stands loyally by Marcius he pleads breathlessly with each disputant in turn, flatters even the loathed Tribunes. But he never loses his head, nor his sense of humor either, gives a savingly comic twist to Marcius' militant

> On fair ground
> I could beat forty of them.

(as indeed we know and see) by his own merry

> I could myself

Take up a brace of the best of them; yea, the two Tribunes.

Nor does he ignore his own side's failings. Of Marcius, momentarily relieved of his incendiary presence:

> His nature is too noble for the world. . . .
> What the vengeance!
> Could he not speak 'em fair?

—into which combination of tempers do these heroes drive us. But here he is at his best, with that frank

> As I do know the Consul's worthiness,
> So can I name his faults.

and in his plea for Rome's honor, threats of death and banishment overhanging the man who has so fought for her:

> Now the good gods forbid
> That our renowned Rome, whose gratitude
> Towards her deserved children is enrolled
> In Jove's own book, like an unnatural dam
> Should now eat up her own! . . .
> What has he done to Rome that's worthy death?
> Killing our enemies, the blood he hath lost—
> Which, I dare vouch, is more than that he hath,
> By many an ounce—he dropped it for his country;
> And what is left, to lose it by his country,
> Were to us all, that do't and suffer it,
> A brand to the end o' the world.

—the artful old man with his crotchets turned to the grave patrician; the verse as fittingly strong and clear.

But to the last moment he is pliably for give-and-take, real or pretended, wailing to his self-wrecked hero a despairing

> Is this the promise that you made your mother?

and past the last moment staying faithfully by him, till he finds place in that sad journey to the gates.

> Thou old and true Menenius,
> Thy tears are salter than a younger man's,
> And venemous to thine eyes.

—yet more quickly dried to calm, it seems. (Here comes one of Shakespeare's incidental touches of veracity.) The fight finished

and lost, the women—Volumnia, even Virgilia—pass from tears
to anger, Menenius to all that is most pacific. There is no more
to be done, and he is very, very weary; though if he

> could shake off but one seven years
> From these old arms and legs . . .

he'd tramp it too by Marcius' side with the best. But Marcius
gone, not even the sight of the swaggering Tribunes rouses him.
Finally, for the distraught and shaken mother and wife he has
nothing but a kindly

> Peace, peace! be not so loud.

unless it be, as Brutus and Sicinius sheer off, the consolation of

> You have told them home,
> And, by my troth, you have cause. . . .

with the yet solider comfort of

> You'll sup with me?

It is unheroic, doubtless, thus to finish such a day. But he is
not heroic!

Tit for tat is hard to resist; nor, certainly, is Menenius a man
to miss a chance of it when it comes. While Marcius is banished
and the Tribunes are in power he keeps a stiff lip in opposition,
foxing enough to warrant their sarcastic

> O! he is grown most kind
> Of late. Hail, sir!

But when the sudden, startling turn of fortune comes, tidings of
Marcius' and Aufidius' dread approach, the old Menenius
reappears, lively and ready as ever:

> What news? what news? . . .
> What's the news? what's the news? . . .
> Pray, now your news? . . .
> Pray, your news?

News suiting his ironic temper in defeat, of the prospect of his
hero's sacking of his city; a pretty contradiction, however deserved.
But here even Menenius' sense of irony will be stretched a little.
He can turn, however, sarcastically on the Tribunes:

> You have made good work,
> You and your apron men. . . .
> You and your crafts! You have crafted fair!

If they shirk the blame, what can the answer to that be but

> How! was't we? ...

But it was.

> We loved him; but, like beasts
> And cowardly nobles, gave way unto your clusters,
> Who did hoot him out o' the city.

And will mere words now win pardon for either lot of them?
Menenius takes delight in assuring the wretched citizens—a troop
of them arriving at this juncture—in assuring them under the
crestfallen Tribunes' very noses that

> not a hair upon a soldier's head
> Which will not prove a whip: as many coxcombs
> As you threw caps up will he tumble down,
> And pay you for your voices.

He once more finds himself, indeed, the old racily tongued
Menenius of our first acquaintance, haranguing the biddable
crowd. Brutus and Sicinius make a last effort to regain their
followers' confidence, but with little enough left in themselves,
it seems. The one-time winners throw in their hands, and the
losers are left to make the best of a bad job between them.

Menenius does not fancy suffering himself the great man's
treatment of Cominius. It was Cominius' business (who preceded
him as Consul) to be the first to go begging forgiveness. Once

> He called me father:
> But what o' that? ...
> Nay, if he coyed
> To hear Cominius speak, I'll keep at home.

But what he wants is to be pressed into going; and for that he
flagrantly plays, until flattery in full measure sends the old man
off, breezily confident that with him to do it the task is as good
as done.

Menenius makes, dramatically speaking, a good end. He plays
the statesman with the soldiers guarding Coriolanus, they, enjoy-
ably, the soldier with him. He is "an officer of state," and he and
Rome, things at the worst, retain, one hopes, their dignity. But
he's not the first to come (here the close-packing of the action,
the tale of Cominius' attempt, adds to the effect of this); and

> our general
> Will no more hear from thence.

Then begins the tussle, familiar to any wartime, between soldier and civilian, the Somebody in peace and Nobody in war, whose condescending

> Good my friends,
> If you have heard your general talk of Rome,
> And of his friends there, it is lots to blanks,
> My name hath touched your ears: it's Menenius.

earns from a sentry under orders no more than a cool

> Be it so; go back: the virtue of your name
> Is not here passable.

Menenius adds to his credit one civilian virtue after another:

> I tell thee, fellow,
> Thy general is my lover: I have been
> The book of his good acts, whence men have read
> His fame unparalleled, haply amplified:
> For I have ever verified my friends,
> Of whom he's chief. . . .

—and it is true!—

> with all the size that verity
> Would without lapsing suffer . . .

each as unavailingly as the last. Indignation does not serve.

> Sirrah, if thy captain knew I were here, he would use me with estimation.
> Come, my captain knows you not.
> I mean thy general.
> My general cares not for you. Back, I say, go; lest I let forth your half-pint of blood. . . .

—the soldier's conclusive argument. Marcius' own appearance, with Aufidius in quiet partnership, puts the matter to the proof.

Nowhere in the play do we find the pattern of its character-planning more effectively turned and colored. The comic charged with emotion; what more human? Old Menenius fatuously insisting upon the sentries discomfiting him, yet heartbroken in his pleading; and it is—we see it—with a cracked heart that Marcius repulses him, that harsh "Away!" little better than a blow in the face. And he must accept Aufidius' praise for it, the dry

> You keep a constant temper.

The sentries allowed their mockery, if they fancy they can out-mock this gallant old patrician in defeat they are vastly mistaken. He can still give back better than he gets:

> I neither care for the world, nor your general: for such things as you, I can scarce think there's any, y'are so slight. . . .

Civilian though he be, he has a weapon of which they cannot rob him:

> He that hath a will to die by himself, fears it not from another. Let your general do his worst. For you, be that you are, long; and your misery increase with your age! [His does!] I say to you, as I was said to, Away!

—and he is gone; bearing off the honors with him, thinks one of these Volscians, duly impressed:

> A noble fellow, I warrant him.

the other of tougher mind:

> The worthy fellow is our general: he's the rock, the oak not to be wind-shaken.

The closely contrived action allows for yet one small turn more in the pattern of character, and typical—fully so—it shall be. The trembling Sicinius awaits tidings; not to be mitigated. But if Menenius has been beaten, let there be no belittling the battle lost; and, if *he* cannot come home winner, who may? Did not Cominius tell them how

> The tartness of his face sours ripe grapes; when he walks he moves like an engine, and the ground shrinks before his treading. . . . He sits in his state, as a thing made for Alexander. . . .

Sicinius may bleat that

> He loved his mother dearly.

Forlornest of hopes, retorted on by

> So did he me; and he no more remembers his mother now than an eight-year-old horse. . . . Mark what mercy his mother shall bring from him: there is no more mercy in him than there is milk in a male tiger. . . .

Menenius, be it remembered, does not know what has passed since his plea was repulsed. For all that he does know it is the right sort of medicine he is administering—having first swallowed it himself with that cheerful courage, which it is lets him in turn so enjoy forcing it down the unhappy Tribune's own throat. Once more comes the solacing refrain:

> and all this is 'long of you.

with, for a closing chord, each striking his own note, Sicinius' pitiful

> The gods be good unto us!

the old politician, gamer:

> No, in such a case the gods will not be good unto us. When we
> banished him we respected not them, and, he returning to break
> our necks, they respect not us.

Take the rough with the smooth and look facts in the face; as wholesome a lesson in politics as lay in the tale of the Belly and the Members. Whereupon, the concluding good news brought and confirmed, Menenius can take this also as coolly—for all that he'll let the two scurvy cowards of Tribunes discover! And with this he is caught back into the ending central stream of the play's action, lively to his last word.

### THE TRIBUNES

Brutus and Sicinius make a listening and a not promptly identifiable first appearance. The aristocrats, assembled by the rumors of war, depart elated, the humiliated citizens steal away, leaving these two—the new Tribunes, will they be?—to savor their comments:

> Was ever man so proud as is this Marcius?
> He has no equal.

They are not of the simple caliber of their followers, that is at once made plain; the craftiest of politicians, rather, with Brutus to belittle—and slander—Marcius, true politician-wise:

> Fame, at the which he aims,
> In whom already he's well-graced, can not
> Better be held nor more attained than by

> A place below the first; for what miscarries
> Shall be the general's fault, though he perform
> To the utmost of a man; and giddy censure
> Will then cry out of Marcius, "O, if he
> Had borne the business!"

Sicinius joining in. The twenty-five-line interchange of cynical judgment stamps them vividly enough on our memory: a binding-up of the story; for between now and our next encounter with them the whole Volscian war is to pass.

We find them again still in Rome (where they are is always Rome); of consequence now, evidently, among the people, but uneasily awaiting the hero's return, decrying him, fearing for their chances beside him. It is now that they take color as comic villains; this thanks to Menenius, who finds ridicule, in which he is bluffly expert, the best weapon with which to torment them. One effect of this will be that while we, with the more sympathetic Menenius, may detest and make fun of them, in other bearings they are still the two sharp politicians. Shakespeare disposes his sides for the coming combat with great address. Here are these two, playing the game by its rules, yielding smoothly to their mastery, condoning no smallest breach of them, pursuing that, indeed, as far and as bitterly as vengeance may. It will be at no point a pretty picture. Set against it we have the cool comment of the neutral Senate House officials upon Marcius as he opens his political career:

> That's a brave fellow; but he's vengeance proud, and loves not the common people.
>
> Faith, there have been many great men that have flattered the people, who ne'er loved them; and there be many that they have loved, they know not wherefore: so that, if they love they know not why, they hate upon no better a ground. Therefore, for Coriolanus neither to care whether they love or hate him manifests the true knowledge he has in their disposition; and out of his noble carelessness lets them plainly see't.

"Noble carelessness"—that phrase alone, with what we have seen of him besides, would weight the sympathy well upon Marcius' side. But the yet cooler, the ironic

> but he seeks their hate with greater devotion than they can render it him . . .

caps it. A political play; the hero, under this aspect of it, with no more skill at the game than makes him his own worst enemy—a fruitful theme. Nor will he take counsel; Menenius could save him more than once. It is between him and the Tribunes that the earlier maneuvering mostly proceeds; Marcius—if he would but let himself be so!—a glorious figurehead, the citizens poor puppets. And it is not so easy to pick holes in the Tribunes' conduct at first. They demand their people's rights: that is only their duty. Is it their fault if Marcius so grudgingly grants these? They slyly incite them to test him at his weakest point. Are they to blame if he not merely yields under the test, but unrepentingly proclaims that here he is, to their despite, at his strongest instead? It is something of a trap, but need he so recklessly walk into it?

But from now on they grow ever more contemptible. They promptly abuse the success they so easily win. Says Marcius scornfully,

> I do despise them;
> For they do prank them in authority
> Against all noble sufferance. . . .
> It is a purposed thing, and grows by plot. . . .

and—though they may safely deny it—we know this is true.

They overplay their hands when they demand Coriolanus' death, show their last sign of political good sense when they'd accept Menenius as mediator in the quarrel. Otherwise they had better have pressed for death, since exile is but to bring back revenge. And something of this they do actually, in the midst of the turmoil, perceive—

> To eject him hence
> Were but one danger, and to keep him here
> Our certain death. . . .

—it being only that their insensate vanity, bred in the flush of success, so blinds them. Marcius gains tragic dignity in defeat and departure; they, tarring the rabble on to hoot him "out at gates," swaggering ludicrously through the streets themselves—"our noble Tribunes"!—touch depth.

When the tide of fortune has turned, although we know what is coming, we see them still sunning themselves fatuously for a while

i' the present peace
And quietness o' the people . . .

Then, foolishly, futilely, denying the plain unpleasant fact,
feebly protesting, when they cannot, against Menenius' mockery.
Nor that the worst. While one still tries, and yet again, to argue
facts away:

*Enter a Messenger.*

Sir, if you'd save your life, fly to your house:
The plebeians have got your fellow-Tribune,
And hale him up and down: all swearing, if
The Roman ladies bring not comfort home,
They'll give him death by inches.

Such politics have their revenges.

# The Action of the Play

*Enter a company of mutinous Citizens, with stones,
clubs and other weapons.*

BUT let not the unwary producer be led by that *mutinous*, and
by the *stones, clubs and other weapons*, into projecting a scene
of mere quick confusion, violence and high-pitched noise. Shakespeare has further reaching intentions. These citizens form a
collective character, so to call it, of capital importance to the first
half of the play; at its very start, therefore, we are to be given a
fully informing picture of them. A homespun lot, but with a man
or so among them that can both think and talk. They are
certainly in an ugly temper at the moment and ripe for mischief,
since plaints and a fortnight's threats have, it seems, proved
futile; and they are not of the breed (Roman or British) that sits
down to starve in patience. So if nothing is left them to do but to
rid themselves and the world of this man they take to be their
"chief enemy," Caius Marcius—why, no more speech-making, nor
parliamentary acclamations of "Resolved, resolved!": let the
thing be done! But they can be halted and made to listen yet once
more. First it is to the chief rebel amongst them ruthfully justi-
fying their intent, protesting that

the gods know I speak this in hunger for bread, not in thirst
for revenge. . . .

then to a last-minute defender Marcius finds among them, bidding them remember the "services he has done for his country." For even though he be "a very dog to the commonalty," all that can be said for him must be heard.

The distant shouts of some kindred company of mutineers rouse them again; such temper is infectious. And they would be off to make common cause with these others; but Menenius Agrippa's arrival once again quiets them. They like old Menenius. He is "one that hath always loved the people." Even the First Citizen will grudgingly admit that

> He's one honest enough: would all the rest were so!

"Honest," perhaps; but little proof of his love for the people is in fact ever forthcoming, and the chief token of his honesty would seem to be that he speaks his mind bluntly to them. But he does so in a sort of rough good fellowship, giving himself no high and mighty airs. How far with them even a show of kindliness will go! He knows how to tackle them. They are his "countrymen," his "good friends," his "honest neighbours"; and within a few minutes he has this mutinous mob quietly gathered round him while he tells them a fairy tale. It is the parable of the Belly and the Members. Only that ruthful rebel the First Citizen is mildly recalcitrant:

> you must not think to fob off our disgrace with a tale. . . .

—which, of course, is just what Menenius means to do. And most readily he does it, going his own leisurely pace, giving the homely humor its full value; and while he holds them there absorbed the mutinous mood ebbs out of them. With the recalcitrant First Citizen he spars offhandedly. A dash of ironic flattery (but indeed the creature is intelligent!), a tolerant snub, flooring him finally amid the merriment of his fellows with a stroke of something less than good-humored ridicule:

> What do you think,
> You, the great toe of this assembly? . . .
> being one o' th' lowest, basest, poorest
> Of this most wise rebellion . . .

After which Caius Marcius himself—Coriolanus to be—strides in. It is for Shakespeare an unusual opening—the plays offer indeed

none comparable to it—with its hundred and sixty lines of
abortive revolt and elaborate parable; he will habitually have
swung his main theme into action within half the time or less.
But it accomplishes a variety of purposes. The mutinous entry
having furnished initial impetus enough, its slackening, the
debate, and their equivocally mild response to Menenius' bluff
bullying, give us a fair view of the citizens not yet in leash to their
Tribunes, a sample of their native quality, upon which the lash of
Marcius' contempt is next so precipitately to fall. The telling of
the parable holds back the action, even as Menenius means it to
hold up the revolt, yet bears directly on it, is no mere digression
(that, at the play's outset, would be a weakness), but enlarges it
at, so to say, one remove. This factor of the citizens and their
condition is thus given ample preparatory display. Marcius'
castigation will cow them now to silence. While the war with the
Volsces is waging they will be absent from the scene. When they
return to it Brutus and Sicinius will be their spokesmen,
maneuvering and coloring their cause for them.

Marcius, abruptly appearing, at once spurs the action to the
swift pace his dominance of it befits. To Menenius' affectionately
admiring tribute of a

> Hail, noble Marcius!

he—though young man to old—returns no more than a curt
"Thanks," so impatient is he to round on the mutineers. Plainly,
Menenius' milder methods have already prevailed; but he must
still vent his spleen. They are rogues and curs, hares in cowardice,
geese in folly, ingrates, their own worst enemies, inconstant and
perverse. They say, do they, that there is grain enough in the city,
yet they are hungry, that though they be dogs, yet dogs must eat?
But

> Would the nobility lay aside their ruth,
> And let me use my sword, I'd make a quarry
> With thousands of these quarter'd slaves, as high
> As I could pick my lance.

Doubtless! And all he says of them and more may be true; but
such scorn for starving fellow-countrymen has no very chivalrous
ring. Nor is Menenius' placatory

> Nay, these are almost thoroughly persuaded;
> For though abundantly they lack discretion,
> Yet are they passing cowardly.

the most generous comment possible upon their surrender to his
wiles. Marcius, it may be, is the angrier with them since the other
"troops," whose shouts we heard, whom he has just quitted, have
by their plaints prevailed with this same nobility to grant them

> a petition . . . a strange one . . .
> Five tribunes to defend their vulgar wisdoms . . .
> S'death!
> The rabble should have first unroofed the city
> Ere so prevailed with me. . . .

He foresees, shrewdly enough, that

> it will in time
> Win upon power and throw forth greater themes
> For insurrection's arguing.

There lies, indeed, the obstacle against which he is to bruise and
break himself, and it is embryonic already in this group of
sullen, silenced, confuted men over which he now rides so
contemptuously roughshod. Marcius is about the least sympathetic
of Shakespeare's heroes, and he is first shown to us in his
unloveliest light.

He is happy to be freed from these cankerous domestic politics
by the sudden news of war:

> we shall ha' means to vent
> Our musty superfluity. . . .

And "our best elders," whose coming follows the news—Cominius
the Consul, old Titus Lartius and other Senators—will have
worthier duties to perform than playing blackmail to the populace.
He himself is consequently in great credit:

> Marcius, 'tis true that you have lately told us;
> The Volsces are in arms.

He can smell the chance of a fight, from wherever the wind of it
blows. And at once, in sharp contrast, he is at his best: his sword
his country's, no questions asked; chivalrous tribute paid to its
chief enemy:

Tullus Aufidius . . .
>                      he is a lion
>        That I am proud to hunt.

It may all go to a somewhat too self-sufficient tune, yet pardonably
stimulated, this—were stimulus needed—by the deference Rome's
great men offer him. He cannot resist, moreover, a parting gibe
at the "worshipful mutiners," become sullenly silent onlookers,
bidding them follow him to play rats among the abundant
Volscian corn, which such a little valor will win. But, says the
stage direction,

> *Citizens steale away.*[11]

(the empty stomach not being one for fighting), while Marcius,
and old Titus, who'd

>        lean upon one crutch and fight with t'other,
>    Ere stay behind this business.

and Cominius the Consul and the Senators, depart high-heartedly
to the Capitol, their place of honor and authority; from it to
proclaim the war.

There have been two other onlookers, silent so far, who now
remain behind: Brutus and Sicinius, the newly appointed
Tribunes. And in the twenty-five lines or so with which they
finish the scene Shakespeare etches them in memorably for the
caustic element in the play they are to prove; politicians sizing up
their destined adversary and, dispassionately, cynically, the weakness and the strength of his position. Nothing to be done now.
They must "wait and see."

## THE VOLSCIANS

The succeeding scene shows us the Senators of Corioles in
council of war, Aufidius bringing news to them of the Roman
preparations, and receiving his commission as general in the
field. The scene is but forty lines long; yet we learn besides that
much "intelligence" passes between Rome and the Volsces—a
point to be made more than once; Rome, civilly distracted, has
her fifth column—and from Aufidius, clinchingly, that

---

11 For the argument that those and other stage directions are Shakespeare's
own, see p. 295ff.

> If we and Caius Marcius chance to meet,
> 'Tis sworn between us we shall ever strike
> Till one can do no more.

The Senators are airily confident:

> Let us alone to guard Corioles. . . .

The clash is nearing.

With the scene which follows all the main factors of the play will have been assembled, and its opening stage direction is illuminating:

## VOLUMNIA AND VIRGILIA

*Enter Volumnia and Virgilia, mother and wife to Marcius.*
*They set them down on two low stools and sew.*

This note of puritan simplicity is struck at once by nothing more elaborate than the two low stools and the sewing. For these are great ladies, and live in state, as the attendant Gentlewoman announcing the Lady Valeria, and the Usher and the Gentlewoman to show her in, will help show us within another minute or so.[12] We remark too the formality of their manners to each other in the "sweet madam," "good madam," "my ladies both," "your ladyship." Volumnia dominates the household. It is to her that Valeria's visit is announced, and Virgilia asks her for permission to retire. Valeria, by contrast, will seem a very frivol; yet it is for a no wilder gaiety she would have Virgilia lay aside her "stitchery" than to "go visit the good lady that lies in."

The scene gives us Volumnia's Spartan temper, harsh at its kindliest, her son's tones—his very words—echoing through hers; Virgilia's gentler spirit, her tremulous courage, her soft stubbornness; Valeria, witty and merry, primed with her news of the war. The opening prose is austere; it paints Volumnia. For the picturing of Marcius in the field comes colored and moving verse. Valeria's chatter about the child brings prose again, easy and decorative, in which medium the scene ends. By reference, Valeria's news:

---

12 For the implicit contrast with the scene between Charmian, Iras, Alexas and the Soothsayer in *Antony and Cleopatra*, see p. 151.

the Volsces have an army forth; against whom Cominius the
general is gone, with one part of our Roman power: your lord
and Titus Lartius are set down before their city Corioles. . . .

advances us several steps in the war; and the next scene's opening:

> *Enter Marcius, Titus Lartius, with drum and colours, with
> Captains and Soldiers, as before the city Corioles.*

with the later

> *Enter two Senators with others on the walls of Corioles.*

## THE WAR WITH THE VOLSCIANS:
### BEFORE CORIOLES

—the walls being simply the upper stage—asks no further
explanation.

The earlier scene has ended with a gentle little tussle between
Valeria and Virgilia, and the gentler of the two has won. Now
begins, under every form of contrast, the man's war. Marcius and
Titus Lartius are in the highest spirits, the old soldier as youthful
as the young, and laying bets—an English trait if not a Roman!—
upon the news the Messenger, just sighted, will be bringing:

> A wager they have met.
> My horse to yours, no?
> 'Tis done.
> Agreed.
> Say, has our general met the enemy?

and, the horse so sportingly lost and won, the bet is then, as
between comrades, generously discounted.

This scene, and the three which follow, are to be predominantly
scenes of action. Marcius is above all a fighting hero, and, most
effectively to warrant him his title, Shakespeare lets us see him
fight. Henry V, Antony, Othello, Macbeth, they also are soldiers;
but—even with Henry V—that is not the aspect of them most
vividly lighted. With Coriolanus, it is his personal prowess in war
and its unlucky linking to as trenchant a pugnacity in peace that
make and mar him. We have heard him for a start at his worst.
We are now to see him at his best, winning valiantly to the
summit of his fortunes. He will thus hold our regard the better
along the descent to his tragic end.

For the battle without its walls, a Roman reverse and recovery, and the taking of Corioles; for a second wavering battle, Marcius to the rescue, and final victory, Shakespeare's material resources are little other than those of the old inn-yard, although doubtless the Globe Theatre at the height of its fame can enrich their quality and be more lavish with them. But *drum and colours* still sufficiently betoken an army on the march, and a recognized code of alarums, trumpet flourishes and the sounding of parleys and retreats illustrate the course of a battle or a siege. It is indeed only by the use of such tokens that the extension and swaying confusions of a battle can be made clear. For with hand-to-hand combat realism's limits are reached.

Shakespeare, using both speech and action, sets his board and makes his moves on it, with exactitude and economy. Marcius and Titus Lartius before Corioles learn that Cominius with his army facing the army of the Volsces are

> Within this mile and half.

Marcius' comment is that

> Then shall we hear their 'larum, and they ours.

When, therefore, a little later we hear the *Alarum afar off*, its meaning is at once plain to us, and distracting explanations are saved. For by then the Senators of Corioles are upon the walls, defying the Romans, and—as drums from within the city help inform us—about to anticipate their assault by a sortie. That Aufidius is not in the city we have at once been told. To the noise of the distant fight is added word that he is a captain in it. Marcius here, then, he there; they are not to meet yet.

> *Enter the army of the Volsces. . . . Alarum. The Romans are beat back to their trenches.*

The hiatus is filled by a seven-line speech from Marcius, both indicating and interpreting the accompanying action:

> They fear us not, but issue forth their city.
> Now put your shields before your hearts, and fight
> With hearts more proof than shields. . . .

That allows, if barely, the symbolic army time to enter and form line, the Romans to start to face them:

> Advance, brave Titus:
> They do disdain us much beyond our thoughts,
> Which makes me sweat with wrath. . . .

—impetuous, impatient!—

> Come on, my fellows:
> He that retires, I'll take him for a Volsce,
> And he shall feel mine edge.

rating them for cowards too, even by anticipation. Fighter but no
leader! Then battle is joined and the Romans are beaten back.[18]
After which

> *Enter Marcius, cursing.*

[18] The ordering of the action upon Shakespeare's stage must be gathered by
piecing together text, stage directions and our yet imperfect and disputed
knowledge of the mechanics of the Globe.

The stage directions are for the most part figurative and recommendatory, not
set down by the book-holder or in his fashion (see p. 295ff.). The curtains to
the inner stage could no doubt be made to serve, but it looks as if this
Corioles had solid gates.

> *Enter the army of the Volsces.*

might, by convention, mean that these opened to discover the dozen men or less
who made the army standing there; and this, for the short time the text allows,
would be convenient. It fits, too, the First Senator's

> our gates,
> Which yet seem shut, we have but pinn'd with rushes;
> They'll open of themselves.

They could—wide enough to let the men through, and close behind them. This
looks likely, and that they reopen later to accommodate the retreat—

> *The Volsces retire into Corioles and Marcius follows them to the gates.*

—and then stay open, to suit Marcius'

> So, *now* the gates are ope: now prove good seconds:
> 'Tis for the followers fortune widens them,
> Not for the fliers. . . .

until they shut on him.

*The Romans are beat back to their trenches* apparently through one of the
side doors, the Volsces following them. It would need to be of some width to
allow for the melee of men, swords and shields, and they might more conveniently
be fought to a standstill on the stage. But *Enter Marcius, cursing,* contradicts this
possibility. He has been beaten off too, the last of the Romans to go. Further,
Titus Lartius is absent when he is shut in the city.

A textual note. In the line

> we'll beat them to their wives,
> As they us to our trenches follows.

(some editors preferring "follow," others "followed"). The "follows" has
probably slipped in by some accident from the neighboring stage direction,
*Marcius follows them to the gates.* Neither sense nor verse accommodates its
speaking.

and the Romans rally; whether thanks to his magnificent vitu-
peration we are free to judge. What is made plain, however, is
that when he calls on them to follow him into the city in pursuit
of the flying enemy—

> mark me, and do the like.

—none of them do. His is no way to win just such devotion from
his soldiers.

> Fool-hardiness; not I!
> Nor I!

And when the gates close on him, for all comment comes a

> See, they have shut him in.

with the grim humor of

> To the pot, I warrant him.

added. Then, Titus Lartius reappearing, Shakespeare stages his
great "effect." The gates open, and there stands Marcius

> *bleeding, assaulted by the enemy.*

alone, at cut and thrust with the whole Volscian "army"; and
the amazing sight, and Titus Lartius' call to them, shame the
recalcitrant Romans—honest fighters enough—into rescuing him,
and so to taking the city.

The stage stays empty for a breathing-space. Then

> *Enter certain Romans, with spoils.*

and we have a three-line tokening of the customary sack of a town:

> This will I carry to Rome.
> And I this.
> A murrain on 't! I took this for silver.

while the

> *Alarum continues still afar off.*

to remind us that Cominius and Aufidius, a "mile and half"
away, are battling still. Marcius and Titus Lartius return,
Marcius fuller than ever of angry scorn for the common soldier,
"these movers . . . these base slaves" that

> Ere yet the fight be done, pack up. Down with them!

he cries, down with these paltry prizes they are pilfering.[14] The
distant alarums continue.

> And hark, what noise the general makes! To him!
> There is the man of my soul's hate, Aufidius,
> Piercing our Romans: then, valiant Titus, take
> Convenient numbers to make good the city;
> Whilst I, with those that have the spirit, will haste
> To help Cominius.

His wounds still bleed. The veteran Titus counsels prudence,
some respite. He will have none of that. He is off. Titus returns
to the city.

The stage is again empty. Then

## COMINIUS' PART OF THE BATTLE

*Enter Cominius, as it were in retire, with soldiers.*[15]

to a very different tempo.

> Breathe you, my friends; well fought! We are come off
> Like Romans, neither foolish in our stands,
> Nor cowardly in retire. . . .

Cominius is Consul and General in Chief, a steady, responsible
soldier; and this has indeed quite the tone of an official bulletin,
issued in mid-battle. For

> believe me, sirs,
> We shall be charged again. . . .

And news of Titus Lartius and Marcius is lacking, and when,
long delayed, it comes, is bad. With clarity and economy
Shakespeare connects the one fight and the other. Cominius has
heard the alarums of the besiegers even as they have heard his.
It is "above an hour" since the Messenger left the Romans "to

---

[14] The *exeunt* occasionally marked for the spoilers after "I took this for
silver" is an editorial interpolation and not in the Folio.

[15] How, in the terms of Shakespeare's theater, is this vacating of the stage,
which marks the end of a scene and change of place, differentiated from that
of a few lines earlier, before the entry of the soldiers with their spoils, which
indicated neither? In the first instance, probably, the open gates still confront us;
in the second, after Titus Lartius and his attendants have passed through them,
not only will they be closed, but the curtain masking the inner stage will be
drawn too.

their trenches driven"; and *we* know what has happened since then, and that Marcius himself is now upon his way here.[16] And when he arrives, so masked in blood that Cominius does not recognize him, we appreciate the effect to the full, since we have already seen him so, and it is as if we had a share ourselves in astonishing Cominius.

No more waiting now, with Marcius here, to be "charged again," if he has aught to say in the matter.

> Where is the enemy? are you lords o' the field?
> If not, why cease you till you are so?

He has left Titus Lartius to do the "mopping-up" in Corioles, is too impatient to be at it again to tell the story of the fight that is over, can scarce spare breath for further railing at "the common file" he so detests. He begs to be set against Aufidius without more delay, and appeals for volunteers to follow him into what must prove a desperate struggle in nobler tones than have sounded from him yet:

> If any such be here,
> As it were sin to doubt, that love this painting
> Wherein you see me smeared; if any fear
> Lesser his person than an ill report;
> If any think brave death outweighs bad life
> And that his country's dearer than himself . . .

and—though momentarily touched by doubt of it when it comes—wins as generous a response.[17] Cominius, we note, without

---

[16] Time, as usual with Shakespeare in such cases, is elastic. We are to picture the Messenger and Marcius dashing across country; so they are allowed likely time for this. As to Titus Lartius' work of making good the city, issuing decrees and the rest of it, that, like the unquestioned minutes of a meeting, we "take as read."

[17] There is corruption of the text hereabouts. When the soldiers take him up in their arms:

> Oh, me alone, make you a sword of me?

has found (to my mind) no very satisfactory interpretation or amendment.

> If these shows be not outward . . .

marks the touch of doubt; and there may be some connection of thought between this and the corrupt line.

Another corruption must be in the line

> Please you to march;
> And four shall quickly draw out my command. . . .

Why "four"? The "Please you to march" is worth noting too, with its unusual suavity.

throwing more doubt upon its zeal, adds solid inducement:

> Make good this ostentation, and you shall
> Divide in all with us.

And so they march—thanks to Marcius, with fresh spirit—to renew the fight.

### BACK TO CORIOLES

*Titus Lartius, having set a guard upon Corioles, going with Drum and Trumpet toward Cominius and Caius Martius, enters with a Lieutenant, other Soldiers and a Scout.*

The scene's action and its seven spoken lines help—and most economically—both to space out and knit together the movements of the siege and the battle as a whole, do so in time and place too. Titus Lartius gives final orders to the Lieutenant for the holding of the town and the sending of reinforcements for the battle still in progress if they are needed. The Lieutenant retires within the gates, which are finally closed; and Titus Lartius with his symbolic Drummer and Trumpeter, the Scout for "guider," and a selection of soldiers takes the road that Marcius more hastily took a while before. The stage is empty again. The curtains before the inner stage (and the gates of Corioles) can now close.

### BACK AGAIN TO COMINIUS' SIDE OF THE BATTLE: CAIUS MARCIUS AND AUFIDIUS MEET

*Alarum as in battle.*

—much such a sound as that which went with the fighting under the walls, the Alarum afar off brought close, and to its most startling and insistent. After which preparation

*Enter Marcius and Aufidius at several doors.*

It is for each the peculiarly critical moment of the day. But before they come to blows they go to it with words, the one out-scorning and outbragging the other. There is something of convention in this, doubtless; but it follows not so much Shakespeare's accustomed "high Roman fashion" as that of Trojan

and Greek in the scurril *Troilus and Cressida*. And it again gives
us Marcius at his crudest, excusable by a certain boyishness in
him, of character if not of years, of the unlicked cub in the man.
Yet it is a flaw of character, which future subtler fighting than
this will fatally widen. Nor is the outcome of this duel to prove
lucky. Clean conquest of his enemy might serve him well. But

> *certain Volsces come in the aid of Aufidius.*

Marcius has little choice but to turn on them, and he

> *fights till they be driven in breathless.*

But for Aufidius to be left (since he can hardly make yet another
in such a melee) to stand there a looker-on, or to follow after
while Marcius so magnificently drives the fellows before him—

> Officious, and not valiant, you have shamed me
> In your condemned seconds.

—will he ever forgive that?[18]

## THE VICTORIOUS ROMAN FORCES
## REASSEMBLE

*Flourish. Alarum. A Retreat is sounded. Enter at one door
Cominius with the Romans: at another door Marcius with
his arm in a scarf.*[19]

The battle is over. The strenuous beat of the action relaxes to

---

[18] Once more Shakespeare, by an incidental stroke, regulates the clock of the
action.

> Within these three hours, Tullus,
> Alone I fought in your Corioles walls. . . .

The echo from *Troilus and Cressida* is in

> Wert thou the Hector
> That was the whip of your bragged progeny. . . .

It may even perhaps echo Hector's own

> You wisest Grecians, pardon me this brag. . . .

[19] So, but for amended spelling, the Folio. Capell, it seems, added . . . *and
other Romans*, and some editors have copied him. But Shakespeare evidently
wishes—be it by an arbitrary effect only—to contrast Cominius and his officers
and men, with the solitary figure of Marcius, once more wounded.

The stage directions hereabouts tend to be emblematic. How precise a meaning
Shakespeare's audience would read into *Flourishes* and *Alarums. A Retreat is
sounded*, and the like, it is hard for us to estimate. A few lines later, moreover,
we have *Enter Titus with his Power from the Pursuit.* Could there have been
any means of illustrating . . . *from the Pursuit?* I fancy this is simple narrative.

the soberer measure of Cominius' stately praise. The threads of
the play's other themes begin at once to be woven back into the
fabric. Cominius, addressing Marcius, speaks of

> the dull Tribunes
> That, with the fusty plebians, hate thine honours . . .

Marcius, in deprecating response, of

> my mother,
> Who has a charter to extol her blood . . .

And here we have him at his best; not too mock-modestly
belittling his own feats, genuinely generous to his comrades:

> I have done
> As you have done; that's what I can; induced
> As you have been; that's for my country:
> He that has but effected his good will
> Hath overta'en mine act.

rejecting reward without a second thought; acknowledging the
supreme honor of

> For what he did before Corioles, call him,
> With all the applause and clamour of the host,
> Caius Marcius Coriolanus! Bear
> The addition nobly ever!

with humorous, becoming simplicity:

> I will go wash;
> And when my face is fair, you shall perceive
> Whether I blush or no: howbeit, I thank you.

Still more attractive is his plea amidst this triumph for the poor
Volscian, some time his host, whose name he only finds himself
too weary now to remember. He wants a drink of wine. And so
we part from him, happy and magnanimous in victory; free too
for the moment—or all but—from that self-conscious egotism
which so besets him.

But the war is not to finish upon this note.

## THE STANDPOINT OF THE VANQUISHED

*A flourish. Cornets. Enter Tullus Aufidius, bloody, with two or three soldiers.*[20]

Here are the defeated Volscians, and the shamed Aufidius. Cominius the Consul in the scene just past had ordered Titus Lartius back to Corioles, and from there to

> send us to Rome
> The best, with whom we may articulate,
> For their own good and ours.

But Aufidius scoffs at confidence in such a peace, in Rome's surrender of the conquered city:

> Condition!
> What good condition can a treaty find
> I' the part that is at mercy? Five times, Marcius . . .

—There it is!—

> I have fought with thee; so often hast thou beat me,
> And wouldst do so, I think, should we encounter
> As often as we eat.

From this sense that he will never now by fair means prove himself the better man springs the mistrust, and hatred, and will the treachery at last to come.

> My valour's poisoned
> With only suffering stain by him. . . .

—the keynote to Aufidius' spiritual tragedy, which time and the event are to work out.


## ROME REJOICES

The entry of Menenius and the Tribunes, Sicinius and Brutus, shows that we are back in Rome. Their acrimonious banter—Menenius an expert at it, the other two doing their humorless best—opens a prospect of the civic war, which is to be rekindled now that the Volscian war is won. But the factors will differ, and

---

[20] It is likelier that *A flourish. Cornets.* rightly belongs to the end of the scene before rather than to the beginning of this, which certainly seems not to call for any sort of "flourish."

the people, with the Tribunes to lead them, prove tougher combatants than before. We have a revaluing of the forces to be engaged, a fresh adjustment of sympathy. Menenius lures the two on. Marcius is blamed for his pride. But

> do you two know how you are censured here in the city, I mean of us o' the right hand file? do you? . . . You talk of pride: O! that you could turn your eyes toward the napes of your necks, and make but an interior survey of your good selves. O! that you could. . . . Why, then you should discover a brace of unmeriting, proud, violent, testy magistrates, alias fools, as any in Rome.

and then, before they can retort on him, he paints his own faults to his liking; an old trick in debate:

> I am known to be a humorous patrician, and one that loves a cup of hot wine with not a drop of allaying Tiber in 't. . . . What I think I utter, and spend my malice in my breath. . . .

with which excuse he goes on to tell them in comically colored terms just what he thinks of them, of their exploiting of the people, and their pretentious folly in general:

> When you speak best unto the purpose, it is not worth the wagging of your beards; and your beards deserve not so honourable a grave as to stuff a botcher's cushion, or to be entombed in an ass's pack-saddle. Yet you must be saying Marcius is proud. . . . God-den to your worships: more of your conversation would infect my brain. . . .

And he turns from them, leaving them glowering, to accost Volumnia, Virgilia, Valeria—a high contrast, in dignity and beauty both—who are hastening across the stage. The news due tonight has come already (Shakespeare's habitual device for sharpening our expectation): the victorious army is approaching, with Marcius, who

> comes the third time home with the oaken garland . . .

Acrid old Menenius transformed to a cheering schoolboy, his cap flung in the air; he and Volumnia, the two elders, competing in extravagant glee; Virgilia and Valeria the staider in joy, Virgilia shrinking from the thought of the wounds

> I' the shoulder and i' the left arm: there will be large cicatrices to show the people when he shall stand for his place. . . .

—this hint of what is to come another habitual device for the sharpening of our expectation. The Tribunes stay glowering in the background; Menenius cannot forbear a passing gibe at them. But suddenly from the distance comes a shout and the sound of trumpets, cutting sharply into the ferment of their jubilation. Volumnia, in a flash, responds; the Roman matron, and inspired:

> Hark the trumpets!
> These are the ushers of Marcius: before him he carries noise,
> and behind him he leaves tears:
> Death, that dark spirit, in's nervy arm doth lie;
> Which, being advanced, declines, and then men die.

A bold and masterly transition; from the familiar and excited prose of the exchanges with Menenius to the portentous trumpet-echoing

> These are the ushers of Marcius. . . .

and the measured music of the conventional "sentence."[21]

> *A sennet. Trumpets sound. Enter Cominius the general, and Titus Lartius; between them Coriolanus, crowned with an oaken garland, with Captains and Soldiers, and a Herald.*[22]

—with all possible pomp and circumstance, that is to say; and dialogue and stage direction now combine to make a notable and most eloquent effect. Nor is it eloquence of words alone;

[21] Shakespeare has been by no means sparing of space in this scene so far. In particular he could have lessened the passage between Menenius and the Tribunes by half and kept all its substance. Is there any reason for this? He may, one suspects, have been sure of an exceptionally good actor for Menenius. Throughout the play he indulges the character and spaciously—in incidental opportunities. Unfounded surmise, no more; but it is somewhat as if he felt he safely could. Another and more technical reason here, if any at all be needed, is at least worth canvassing. We have left Marcius bloody and unkempt after his fighting. The actor must have time to put himself in proper array for his triumphal entry. Will the speaking of 190 lines allow him more than enough? And here the question of act-division—between I and II—is also involved. Is this Shakespeare's, or an editor's? And if Shakespeare's, and to be marked in performance, was an appreciable interval allowed or no? Speculative questions, and of no capital importance; pertaining to the play's study, nevertheless. For the main question of act-division, see p. 294ff.

[22] *Titus Lartius?* A slip, apparently, on Shakespeare's part. Menenius tells us later that he has been sent for, and, a scene later still, he arrives, to be questioned by Coriolanus about Tullus Aufidius and the Volscian preparation for revenge.

Shakespeare's stagecraft has outpassed that. Ringing speech pertains to the Herald:

> Know, Rome, that all alone Marcius did fight
> Within Corioles gates. . . .
> Welcome to Rome, renowned Coriolanus!

and to the response, in unison, of the nameless onlookers:

> Welcome to Rome, renowned Coriolanus!

The flow of sound—trumpets, the Herald's trenchant tones, the volume of voices—suddenly ceasing, creates, so to speak, a silence in which Coriolanus' or Volumnia's simplest phrase, spoken in all simplicity, will tell to the height of its value.

> No more of this; it does offend my heart:
> Pray now, no more.

he begs them. The distaste is again genuine, barely tainted by mock-modesty. But the self-consciousness which sets him so continually insisting on it shows a crack in character, if a slight one.

The three women, becomingly, do not press forward; this, to the end, is soldiers' business. Cominius himself must intervene with a

> Look, sir, your mother!

And Marcius steps from his place of honor to kneel to her. For once her sterner self dissolves in emotion. There is tenderness in the pride of the

> Nay, my good soldier, up . . .

and thereupon he is her "gentle" Marcius, her "worthy" Caius, the pride returning almost shyly in the

> What is't? Coriolanus must I call thee?

as if she scarce dare trust the gloriously earned title on her tongue. Then she yields her mother's claim to the wife's.

Virgilia stands quietly, happily, crying. Marcius, to mask his own emotion at their reuniting, rallies her with a loving, but half-humorous

> My gracious silence, hail!

with the gentle irony of

> Wouldst thou have laughed had I come coffin'd home,
> That weep'st to see me triumph? . . .

The thought follows:

> Ah, my dear,
> Such eyes the widows in Corioles wear,
> And mothers that lack sons.

none better befitting the poignant gravity of such a triumph. It is Marcius' noblest moment.

Menenius recalls them to their rejoicings. These center on this group of the people of consequence in Rome, exchanging greetings, so content with themselves and their world. Says Marcius:

> Ere in our own house I do shade my head
> The good patricians must be visited. . . .

He ignores, that is to say, the Tribunes, although Menenius, with another merry gibe, points them out to him. Volumnia voices more positively now her high hopes of the consulship for him. His response is cold. Then *Flourish. Cornets. . .* , and the procession, Volumnia and Virgilia joined to it, passes on its way, leaving the neglected Brutus and Sicinius to discuss the situation.[23]

First, Brutus must vent his spleen. And if the coloring of his picture of Rome's greeting to her hero is dyed deep in jealousy of Marcius, it reflects contempt too for the people whose champion he is, as little kindness for "the kitchen malkin" who

~~~~~~~~~~

[23] There is an inconsistency in the stage directions here to be noted. The Folio marks an *Enter Brutus and Sicinius*, having accorded them no certain *exeunt*. Nothing very out of the way in this; both Folio and Quartos abound in such apparent slips. But it opens up a question of the movements and the placing of the two during the interchange between Menenius and Volumnia, and next while Marcius dominates the scene. They are still there, of course, when Menenius addresses them with his

> God save your good worships! Marcius is coming home.

But are they when he cites them to Marcius for the

> old crab-trees here at home that will not
> Be grafted to your relish. . . .

If not, but for a responsive shrug or the like, Marcius neglect of them will be purely negative. It looks, however, as if they were intended still, at this moment, to be thereabouts, glowering in the background. And probably they go off with the procession, hang back from it, and immediately return. This will at least justify the Folio's stage direction and give point to Brutus' sequent speech, his description of the hero's greeting by the crowd.

pins

> Her richest lockram 'bout her reechy neck,
> Clambering the walls to eye him . . .

as for the "seld-shown flamens" who "press among the popular throngs" and "our veiled dames" with "their nicely-gawded cheeks." A man of no rose-tinted illusions, Brutus, except, possibly, about himself!

Sicinius has his mind on realities. In a dry seven words he states them:

> On the sudden
> I warrant him Consul.

and Brutus, rancor indulged, is as shrewd:

> Then our office may,
> During his power, go sleep.

Very coolly the two then canvass the prospect: Marcius' failings,

> He cannot temperately transport his honours. . . .

—the unstable temper of the commoners, which, in his pride, he is sure soon to provoke again. So

> At some time when his soaring insolence
> Shall touch the people—which time shall not want,
> If he be put upon't; and that's as easy
> As to set dogs on sheep—will be his fire
> To kindle their dry stubble; and their blaze
> Shall darken him for ever.

They themselves have but meanwhile to "suggest" to the people—the word is twice used—

> in what hatred
> He still hath held them . . .

and wait, not for long.

The scene ends upon a Messenger's summoning them to the Capitol, for

> 'Tis thought
> That Marcius shall be Consul. . . .

and he breaks, his commission done, into a rapturous

> I have seen the dumb men throng to see him, and
> The blind to hear him speak: matrons flung gloves,

> Ladies and maids their scarfs and handkerchers,
> Upon him as he passed; the nobles bended,
> As to Jove's statue, and the commons made
> A shower and thunder with their caps and shouts:
> I never saw the like.

It is Brutus' tale again, but by this young hero-worshiper how differently told; its enthusiasm gall to the hearers, who, bracing themselves for the coming struggle, depart.

## MARCIUS' FIRST STEP IN POLITICS

So much for the hero's greeting by his patrician equals and by the populace. Shakespeare now provides a passing comment on him from a third standpoint..

> *Enter two Officers, to lay cushions, as it were, in the Capitol.*[24]

Here is—to modernize it somewhat—the permanent official's detached view of the politician, with its somewhat cynically critical discrimination. Coriolanus is

> a brave fellow; but he's vengeance proud, and loves not the common people.

Who, then, in Rome will not say that of him? Detached analysis follows:

> there hath been many great men that have flattered the people, who ne'er loved them; and there be many that they have loved, they know not wherefore: so that if they love they know not why, they hate upon no better a ground. Therefore, for Coriolanus neither to care whether they love or hate him manifests the true knowledge he has in their disposition; and out of his noble carelessness lets them plainly see it.

True enough, and "noble carelessness" no doubt becomes a hero. But, comes the answer, is it only that?

---

[24] *To lay cushions, as it were* . . . is one among the play's "suggestive" stage directions. A cushion can mean "the seat of a judge or ruler" (though the reference for this definition in the O.E.D. is dated 1659). Presumably the officers have a couple of actual cushions, or more, to lay. But the phrase has, I fancy, a further implication; it tells us—even as the subsequent dialogue shows—the sort of persons they are, not menials, but men of a definite dignity, the equivalent, possibly, in Shakespeare's mind, to officers of Parliament, who may bring to their covenanted respect for its members, Lords or Commons, a very critical private view of their individual worth.

he seeks their hate with greater devotion than they can render in him, and leaves nothing undone that may fully discover him their opposite. Now, to seem to affect the malice and displeasure of the people is as bad as that which he dislikes, to flatter them for their love.

"He seeks their hate. . . ." Shrewd comment! And it is the seamy side of this aspect of the man, the impulse which sets him upon his road to disaster. For his defense:

> He hath deserved worthily of his country. . . .

and not to let such deeds excuse his faults were gross ingratitude. Finally, "He's a worthy man"; on that they agree. Again—and here upon the verge of the action's chief struggle—Shakespeare has trimmed the balance of its sympathies.

> *Sennet. Enter, with Lictors before them, Cominius the consul, Menenius, Coriolanus, Senators, Sicinius and Brutus. The Senators take their places; the Tribunes take theirs by themselves. Coriolanus stands.*

The Lictors before the Consul, the Senators and Tribunes in their respective places, Coriolanus standing facing them, as one about to be harangued—this paints the occasion accurately enough; and Menenius' opening

> Having determined of the Volsces, and
> To send for Titus Lartius, it remains,
> As the main point of this our after-meeting . . .

enlarges the circumstances, and, by suggestion, lengthens the apparent time events have been taking, lending them more reality.[25]

Marcius is to be publicly thanked for his "noble service" to the State. The question of the consulship, which is in everyone's

---

[25] At Cominius' command the procession moved "on to the Capitol." Brutus and Sicinius, after a fifty-five-line talk, are summoned there also, because

> 'Tis thought
> That Marcius shall be Consul.

and the thirty-five-line talk between the Officers lets them arrive in time for the business. Menenius' "This our after-meeting . . ." implies that more has been happening, and associates the public thanks to Coriolanus and his proposal as Consul with the general business of the State, and lends them verisimilitude and importance thereby.

mind, will be canvassed later, and with no voice to the contrary, supposedly, and so hard upon the praise with which Cominius will crown his triumph. Wherefore the Senators' confident request to the Tribunes, as "Masters o' the people," for their "kindest care," and their

> loving motion toward the common body,
> To yield what passes here.

But parliamentary courtesy between the parties is even now at a strain. Note Sicinius' canting

> We are convented
> Upon a pleasing treaty, and have hearts
> Inclinable to honour and advance
> The theme of our assembly.

continued smoothly into Brutus' sarcastic

> Which the rather
> We shall be blest to do, if he remember
> A kinder value of the people than
> He hath hereto prized them at.

and Menenius' temper tetchily shortening with these "Masters o' the people" ("*your* people"—he cannot disguise his contempt). And while Cominius, ready with his Consular speech, is thus kept waiting, Coriolanus himself, hero of the occasion, declaring that

> I had rather have one scratch my head i' the sun
> When the alarum were struck than idly sit
> To hear my nothings monstered.

hardly improves it by abruptly departing. Altogether, an unpromising beginning to a political career!

But Cominius' speech, its recalling of what this man has done for Rome, must surely obliterate all petty differences about him. Says the chief Senator:

> He cannot but with measure fit the honours
> Which we devise him.

And when, brought back, Menenius announces to him without more ado:

> The Senate, Coriolanus, are well pleased
> To make thee Consul.

there is at least no dissentient voice. The business being on the crest of the wave, then, he adds at once—a monitory hint to Marcius, one fancies, in his tone:

> It then remains
> That you do speak to the people.

But—as is to be expected—without a moment's heed comes back the

> I do beseech you
> Let me o'erleap that custom. . . .[26]

and Sicinius is as quick with his

> Sir, the people
> Must have their voices; neither will they bate
> One jot of ceremony.

Menenius, however, all conciliation in success, would be closing the gap:

> Put them not to 't;
> Pray you, go fit you to the custom. . . .

And the self-conscious Marcius'

> It is a part
> That I shall blush in acting. . . .

is a yielding plea—were that all. But he must needs add:

> and might well
> Be taken from the people.

and play into the Tribunes' hands. Brutus'

> Mark you that!

is exultant. To cover the blunder and halt the dangerous argument, Menenius and the Senators, without more delay, in due form recommend him Consul to the Tribunes, through them to the people, themselves, moreover, positively acclaiming him:

---

[26] "Without a moment's heed . . .": this is sufficiently indicated in the continuity of the verse. Marcius' "I do beseech you . . ." completing Menenius' line. Besides which (the actor will remember) Brutus has

> heard him swear,
> Were he to stand for Consul, never would he
> Appear i' the market-place, nor on him put
> The napless vesture of humility . . .

> to our noble Consul
> Wish we all joy and honour.

—and every voice in the Senate answers

> To Coriolanus come all joy and honour!

It is one of the play's salient and most significant moments. Marcius has sworn (Brutus says he heard him, reiterates, "It was his word") that never, to be chosen Consul, will he stand in the market place, show his wounds and beg the people's voices. Yet plainly he now means, after a little persuasion, to do so. Shakespeare will not, in other words, bring him to grief upon a point of mere stubbornness and vanity. And the Tribunes would so far be facing defeat did he not in the very same breath—and how gratuitously!—open up the larger quarrel. Such a privilege

> might well
> Be taken from the people.

Thus jauntily he throws the gauntlet down. It is upon what grows from this, issues of statecraft, nothing petty and egotistic—however egotistically and arrogantly he may urge them—that he will take his stand, and will fail. Here is indeed the play's turning point, from which it develops into true tragedy, with Marcius' character, given that scope, itself rising to heroic stature.

The political war ahead, in which Coriolanus is to be worsted, asks for other qualities than those which so well served in him to beat the Volsces. Brutus and Sicinius will prove to be the successful generals now, and their tactics are to await for the while the adversary's errors. The Senators and their hero departed; says Brutus,

> You see how he intends to use the people.

And they set off themselves to anticipate Coriolanus in the market place and do what may seem wise to bias the proceedings there.[27]

~~~~~~~~~~

[27] But here Shakespeare performs one of his occasionally convenient feats of sleight of hand. The Tribunes quit the stage with this intention; but immediately after the citizens enter, as in the market place, expecting Marcius, who shortly arrives. There has been no opportunity, then, for interference by the Tribunes—unless some break in the continuity of the action, some imaginary passage of time between the two scenes is to be conceded, and that can be counted out of

## THE TROUBLES IN THE MARKET PLACE BEGIN

*Enter seven or eight Citizens.*

In the few lines spoken before Marcius appears we renew acquaintance with them, and sample their present mood.

> Once, if he do require our voices, we ought not to deny him.

—the First Citizen is quite positive about it.[28] The Second Citizen insists on their rights:

> We may, sir, if we will.

The Third Citizen enjoys arguing things out, and the sound of words, and, possibly, of his own voice:

> We have power in ourselves to do it, but it is a power that we
> have no power to do. . . . Ingratitude is monstrous, and for the

the question. Moreover, there is no sign in the talk of the citizens among themselves, or to Marcius, that Brutus and Sicinius have recently been at them. Yet, arriving later, when the ordeal is over and the "voices" have been accorded, the two pointedly refer to the good advice they gave, and scold their already disillusioned followers for neglecting it.

> Could you not have told him
> As you were lessoned . . . ?
> Thus to have said,
> As you were fore-advised . . .

We probably do not detect the trick. But what brings Shakespeare to playing it? Is it that, having dispatched the Tribunes (so to say) to the market place, he sees how much better it may be to let the citizens encounter Marcius in his "gown of humility" without their interference? Yet there is value in the present subsequent passage in which they expound and deplore the errors . that, all against their advice, have been made, and undertake to relieve them. For it is in this that they give evidence of being "masters o' the people" indeed. It will then become important not to prejudice its effect by staging shortly beforehand a similar passage of the actual giving of the good advice. Very well; that can be omitted, advantageously from other points of view also. And if it is also important to have the Tribunes reproach the citizens for ignoring their advice, let them do so. We are unlikely to remark later that the advice was never given, nor, as the action ran, could have been.

28 I doubt if any consistency of character can be established between the First or Second Citizens of the play's opening and of this scene, or between them in this and any of the later ones. Within the boundary of a single scene there will be consistency; they will be ineffectual figures otherwise. But to push the matter further would be to make each a character in his own right, so to speak, and to rob the populace of its collective strength. No matter how diverse the opinions and feelings to be vented, a crowd must remain dramatically a single if a multiple unit.

multitude to be ingrateful were to make a monster of the multitude. . . .

They are not forgetful:

> for once we stood up about the corn, he himself stuck not to call us the many-headed multitude.

Yet they bear no malice; let bygones be bygones.

> if he would incline to the people, there was never a worthier man.

—upon which Marcius appears, as demanded, in the gown of humility, shepherded by a Menenius who is plainly most apprehensive of what may happen when in a moment his fatherly and restraining influence is withdrawn.

As with the scenes of battle, the passages which now follow between Coriolanus and the citizens are as eloquent, or all but, in their action as in their speech; and disposition and movement ask careful perceiving. Both parties at first shirk the encounter. The citizens, at the sight of the man who has heretofore never met with them but to abuse them, herd together for mutual support, until the sapient Third Citizen protests that

> We are not to stay all together, but to come to him where he stands, by ones, by twos and by threes. . . .

and stiffens their backs a bit. And Coriolanus, that bold fighter, at his most miserably self-conscious as he shows himself in the detested gown, would bolt, it seems, from these despised boors if he might, like a shy schoolboy. There is a generous measure of the comic in the scene, contributed by no means by its simpletons only. Shakespeare does not scruple now, should it suit him, to add to a tragic hero's diet a taste or two of the bitter sauce of ridicule.

Coriolanus takes his stand, to await assault. It is a queer caricature of the picture we so recently had of him, fighting "all alone . . . within Corioles gates." He now has instead of Volsces these kindly fumbling fellow Romans, offering him a victory which the arrogant demon in him does everything to spurn. Fatherly Menenius is in despair:

> You'll mar all:
> I'll leave you: pray you, speak to 'em, I pray you,
> In wholesome manner.

and Marcius' response is certainly not reassuring:

> Bid them wash their faces,
> And keep their teeth clean.

—let them hear it if they like; what does he care![29]

It looks, indeed, an embarrassing business enough: the hero, stripped of his martial trappings, his oaken garland, and appearing, it must be owned, a little ridiculous in this gown of humility. Not so ridiculous as he himself fears, and in the eyes of these simple, serious-minded citizens, not at all. But Marcius, his martial glory disregarded, has not—it is the fatal flaw—the humane and inward dignity which can outshine appearances.

It is distressing, also, to see him so smartly sparring at these simple folk, unable to resist the puzzling repartee, the adroit seizing of a vantage-point, the covert insolence. One gentle stroke pierces his harness. The Third Citizen has ventured the artlessly cunning, joke-in-earnest of

> You must think, if we give you anything, we hope to gain by you.

upon which Marcius pounces with

> Well then, I pray, your price o' th' consulship?

Says the First Citizen very quietly:

> The price is to ask it kindly.

That goes home. It does not soften him. He is no sentimentalist. But at least he next responds as one man allowably may to another—

> Kindly! Sir, I pray, let me ha't: I have wounds to show you, which shall be yours in private. Your good voice, sir; what say you?

—if, even so, he cannot keep derision from his tones, inverted arrogance from the concluding

> I have your alms. Adieu!

---

[29] A point obscured in most modern editions by their setting the entrance of the citizens after the line has been spoken, whereas the Folio has them enter just before. It does not follow that he definitely intends them to hear it; he does not see them until immediately after. But they were there a moment before; he knows they are about. The point is that he does not care.

They have not the wit nor the wish to retort on him in kind. But they are none the less conscious of his mockery, and resentment will secrete in them only the more abundantly.

These three are replaced by a Fourth Citizen and a Fifth, the Fourth plain-spoken:

> You have deserved nobly of your country, and you have not deserved nobly. . . . You have been a scourge to her enemies, you have been a rod to her friends; you have not indeed loved the common people.

The candidate counters with irony:

> You should account me the more virtuous that I have not been common in my love. . . .

But by all means, if they prefer it, he will flatter his

> sworn brother the people, to earn a dearer estimation of them . . . practise the insinuating nod . . . counterfeit the bewitchment of some popular man, and give it bountiful to the desirers. . . .

Could he—were they not such impervious clods!—do more positively to induce them to reject him? Nor will he frankly show these two his wounds; only, since he must, beg them for their "voices"—which they promise him "heartily." He is then left a breathing-space.

Marcius is no more given to reasoning coolly with himself than with others. Inward conviction is his only strength; and, erring against it, as he is erring now, he becomes like an animal caught in a net, frantic, struggling, self-strangled.

> Better it is to die, better to starve . . .

—by test of reason, certainly, a somewhat overcharged outburst. The protest against custom's tyranny,

> What custom wills, in all things should we do't,
> The dust on antique time would lie unswept,
> And mountainous error be too highly heaped
> For truth to o'erpeer. . . .

comes with unconscious irony from the conservative mind in rebellion. But, having brought himself thus far to "fool it so"—

> I am half through;
> The one part suffered, the other will I do.

—resentment would seemingly fade into shrugging self-contempt, did there not at this point

*Enter three Citizens more.*

The sight of them stirs him to a very self-scourging of mockery:

> Your voices! For your voices I have fought;
> Watched for your voices; for your voices bear
> Of wounds two dozen odd; battles thrice six
> I have seen and heard of. . . .

But, their own stolid simplicity unaffected, the scourge flags, the mockery peters out—

> for your voices have
> Done many things, some less, some more: your voices. . . .

—into the final surrender of

> Indeed, I would be Consul.

That he should come to this! They give him his reward:

> He has done nobly. . . . Therefore let him be Consul. . . . God
> save thee, noble Consul!

and as Menenius returns, the Tribunes with him, these simple folk inconspicuously depart; Marcius, released, venting an incorrigible

> Worthy voices![30]

Menenius is triumphant. His man wins; and the rest of the business can be pushed through without more delay. Sicinius stiffly assents. Marcius only demands: will it be decently done in the Senate House, not here in the vulgar market place; and

> May I change these garments?

—this ridiculous "gown of humility"? He may. Then all's well; and he and Menenius both are off in high feather. Diplomatic Menenius does not forget to ask their good colleagues the Tribunes to go along with them. No; they prefer to "stay here for the people"; their people. Sicinius' smooth "Fare you well" has an inauspicious ring.

Brutus thinks all is lost for the time being, and would dismiss

---

[30] For the technical treatment of this soliloquy, see the section upon the play's verse, p. 276ff.

the people. Sicinius will wait and see. And, sure enough, when
the plebeians reassemble, the tide of their favor towards Marcius
is already on the turn. Did he suppose, because they did not
retort then and there, that they were insensible to his sarcasm?

> To my poor unworthy notice,
> He mocked us when he begged our voices.

says the Second Citizen; and the Third, thus encouraged:

> Certainly.
> He flouted us downright.

But attack again brings defense. The First Citizen, in a minority
of one though he may be, stands out:

> No, 'tis his kind of speech; he did not mock us.

As in that old quarrel over the corn, Marcius must have fair play.

Brutus and Sicinius know better than to join in the attack while
it is strong enough without them. There are better ways of
fomenting it. Surely he can never have refused—Sicinius won't
believe it—his fellow citizens their right to see

> His marks of merit, wounds received for 's country.

The Third Citizen is effectively roused:

> He said he had wounds, which he could show in private;
> And with his hat, thus waving it in scorn,
> "I would be consul," says he: "aged custom,
> But by your voices, will not so permit me;
> Your voices therefore."

Not a derisive phrase nor a scornful twist of the tongue did he
miss, it seems:

> When we granted that,
> Here was, "I thank you for your voices: thank you:
> Your most sweet voices: now you've left your voices
> I have no further with you." Was not this mockery?

The rest mutely agree. They have behaved like fools. The
Tribunes now read them—and not for the first time, upon this
very subject!—a sound political lesson.[31]

Admitting that his recent "worthy deeds" gave him a claim

---

[31] "Not for the first time": see p. 211, note 27.

upon them, they should have reminded him of his ancient enmity towards them. Clearly, they should have said, they could not risk his remaining a "fast foe to the Plebeii." They should indeed have demanded from him a pledge for his future good behavior—which, if he had given it, they could have held him to; and if, as was more likely, the mere demand had "galled his surly nature," then, "putting him to rage," they could have

> ta'en the advantage of his choler,
> And passed him unelected.

For do they suppose that a man who can treat them as he has now done when he needs their votes will prove very considerate when he no longer needs them? And are they, who have " 'ere now denied the asker"—the candid, honest asker—to bestow their "sued-for tongues" in thanks for such treatment as this? The appeal is to sound sense and self-respect. And it needs but a single evasive

> He's not confirmed; we may deny him yet.

to stampede the rest:

> And will deny him:
> I'll have five hundred voices of that sound.

And the rot will spread:

> I twice five hundred and their friends to piece 'em.

Brutus has the demagogue's sense of a crowd's mood and the critical moment:

> Get you hence instantly, and tell those friends,
> That they have chosen a Consul that will from them take
> Their liberties. . . .

—rate them for fools as we are rating you. But Sicinius is for putting a more temperate face on the affair:

> Let them assemble,
> And, on a safer judgment, all revoke
> Your ignorant election. . . .

—let them confess it to be so. Then he builds them up their case; against Marcius' pride, and his old hatred of them, which in the light of his great deeds they had been so ready to forget as not to note the mocking scorn, sure sign that he hated them still. Upon which draft Brutus is quick to improve:

> Lay
> A fault on us, your Tribunes, that we laboured—
> No impediment between—but that you must
> Cast your election on him.

A brilliant maneuver from the Tribunes' standpoint! The people will save their faces, and they win credit for a patriotic effort to heal this old unhappy quarrel. So excellent seems the notion that they enlarge on it until they find themselves lauding, not Marcius alone, but his ancestors also for their services to Rome and its people; very practical, popular services; for

> Of the same house Publius and Quintus were,
> That our best water brought by conduits hither. . . .

So Sicinius must steer back to the point, that

> you have found . . .
> That he's your chief enemy, and revoke
> Your sudden approbation.

while Brutus encourages them again with another

> Say you ne'er had done it—
> Harp on that still—but by our putting on. . . .

for already the tide of their resentment has ebbed to the uncertainty of an

> *almost* all
> Repent in their election.

But they depart to do the bidding of these political masters, who linger a moment, themselves, before taking their shorter way to the Capitol, to reflect that, mildly as it yet promises,

> This mutiny were better put in hazard
> Than stay, past doubt, for greater. . . .

and that, arriving "before the stream of the people," the threat of it can be made to

> seem, as partly 'tis, their own,
> Which we have goaded onward.

## THE BATTLEGROUND IS BEFORE THE
## CAPITOL NOW

*Cornets. Enter Coriolanus, Menenius, all the Gentry,
Cominius, Titus Lartius, and other Senators.*

*All the Gentry* is to be noted, with the completeness of the
contrast it indicates between this gathering and that of the homespun group of citizens. The cornets, elaborately sounding, tell
us that the ceremonies of the election are not yet over. Coriolanus
is once more fitly attired for them. And he is already deferred
to as Consul—Titus Lartius, back from Corioles, but still in
fighting trim, calls him "my lord"; Cominius addresses him as
"Lord Consul"—and spontaneously, confidently, so asserts himself. He nurses no illusions, as the more pacific Cominius does,
that Rome has finished with the Volscians, points a prompt finger
towards the source of trouble to come with his

> Saw you Aufidius?

is as boyishly himself as ever in the eager

> Spoke he of me? . . .
>                How? What?

Aufidius has retired to Antium, has he, there to bide his time?
This by triple repetition is impressed on us. Then, says Marcius:

> I wish I had a cause to seek him there. . . .

—and the words will lodge in our memory.

So here is Coriolanus on the very crest of the wave, Rome's
leader elect, and just such a leader as she may most need, with
war, as is hinted, likely to threaten her again. Supported by the
Senate and the gentry, he is now on his way back from the Capitol
to the market place for the final act of the election, the people's
confirmation of their acceptance of him. The Tribunes enter as
from the market place. They do not speak at once; and Marcius
apparently is not unwilling that, as they stand there, they should
overhear his comments on them:

> Behold, these are the tribunes of the people,
> The tongues o' the common mouth: I do despise them;

> For they do prank themselves in authority,
> Against all noble sufferance.[32]

The Tribunes do not mean to be provoked into losing their tempers. They are come, on the contrary, to prevent disorder. Coriolanus must not proceed to the market place:

> The people are incensed against him.

Brutus confirming Sicinius with a solemn

>                                    Stop,
> Or all will fall in broil.

Coriolanus, needless to say—and the Tribunes have counted on it—flares into anger at once, and first against the Tribunes themselves for failing to control their "herd":

> What are your offices?
> You being their mouths, why rule you not their teeth?

"Rule"—the first thought to his mind; and a minute later he is inveighing against

>                         such as cannot rule
> Nor ever will be ruled.

(Brutus and Sicinius could tell him if they would that while they get their own way with their "herd"—and better than he knows how to—it is not by rule.)

His tactic, in this sort of fight as in another, is at once to force the acutest issue:

> Have you not set them on?

—let them deny it if they can. Theirs is to lure him aside. The vexed, one-time question about the corn, Brutus neatly casts that into the arena. Marcius scoffs:

> Why, this was known before.

and—the quarrel then widening to admit Cominius and Menenius to a share in it—one hopes he may have the sense to drop the subject. But no!

> Tell me of corn!
> This was my speech, and I will speak 't again—

---

[32] If he is not at least willing for them to overhear, there is little or no point in the lines. But here is the schoolboy side of him, very similarly shown in the scene of the gown of humility.

and not Menenius nor the Senators can stay him.

Nor is this the worst. Though his friends beseech him not to, he must needs go on to raise the whole question of these privileges that have been granted to "the mutable, rank-scented meynie"— political disapproval and personal fastidiousness combined!—for

> I say again,
> In soothing them we nourish 'gainst our Senate
> The cockle of rebellion, insolence, sedition,
> Which we ourselves have ploughed for, sowed and scattered,
> By mingling them with us, the honoured number. . . .

Brutus' acid comment,

> You speak o' the people
> As if you were a god to punish, not
> A man of their infirmity.

is a not altogether surprising one.

Marcius had been ready with this protest, and was fended by but a little from making it, upon the verge of the prescribed appeal in the gown of humility on the market place. In hot blood he has, to their faces, denounced the people yet more fiercely; and Menenius urges the Tribunes not, in fairness, to take advantage of his choler now. Marcius consents to no such excuse:

> Choler!
> Were I as patient as the midnight sleep,
> By Jove, 't would be my mind.

And it is at this juncture that, a graver note sounding, we become aware of him grown to more heroic stature, to take his stand for a cause of greater import than his own:

> O good, but most unwise patricians! why,
> You grave but reckless Senators, have you thus
> Given Hydra here to choose an officer. . . ?

For of two things one: the hydra-headed people will rule, or he— this Sicinius or the like—in their name; and

> If he have power,
> Then veil your ignorance; if none, awake
> Your dangerous lenity. If you are learned,
> Be not as common fools; if you are not,
> Let them have cushions by you. You are plebeians,
> If they be Senators: and they are no less. . . .

> By Jove himself,
> It makes the Consuls base: and my soul aches
> To know, when two authorities are up,
> Neither supreme, how soon confusion
> May enter 'twixt the gap of both and take
> The one by the other.

—it is a note never sounded by Marcius before; the rare note of selfless intellectual passion.

This is the juncture too at which he begins to alienate his friends. Little do the Senators want less—they are as apt politicians as the Tribunes—than to have such an issue raised. Cominius would evade it with a

> Well, on to the market place.

But that only sets this incorrigible Consul-elect to prove his case by revising the well-worn quarrel about the corn—and, since he will, why, adroitly he argues it as could the most proficient politician of them all. And that brings him to lashing at the people yet once more for their wartime cowardice, and Menenius cannot stop him.

He finds himself at last upon the higher ground again, for him the highest. What can go well in a state

> where gentry, title, wisdom,
> Cannot conclude but by the yea and no
> Of general ignorance . . .

Even for the people's own sake

> at once pluck out
> The multitudinous tongue; let them not lick
> The sweet which is their poison. . . .

Dangerous ground! Brutus and Sicinius have no more need of their façade of indignation. It sputters from them:

> Has said enough.
> Has spoken like a traitor, and shall answer
> As traitors do.

But it is not in Marcius to retreat. Here, indeed, he is, in the sort of situation that most delights him, singlehanded against odds, reckless of consequence. And with the happy, schoolboy ribaldry of the question:

What should the people do with these bald Tribunes. . . ?

he is ready to

> throw their power i' the dust.

Not for this was he to be elected Consul. It is, as Brutus says, "Manifest treason." But revolutions do not always come from below.

Such a quarrel started, each must line up on his own side. And the summoning of the Aediles to apprehend Rome's hero

> as a traitorous innovator,
> A foe to the public weal . . .

—the Tribunes will carefully keep their law-abiding and conservative footing—rallies the troubled Senate round him.[33] Sicinius, violently excited, is for arresting Marcius with his own hands; Cominius, scandalized, protesting; Marcius, at his senile touch, with a

> Hence, rotten thing, or I shall shake thy bones
> Out of thy garments.

sending him yelping off in terror. Hullaballoo ensues; Coriolanus alone standing silent and unmoved.

The first thing is to quiet it; and this only the Tribunes, who have roused it, can well do. Menenius, outshouted, helpless, is reduced to begging "good Sicinius" to speak to the people. If he thinks he has a peacemaker in him he is much mistaken. Sicinius but repeats quietly and more clearly what he has already called aloud:

---

[33] There is significance in the two stage directions: first

*Enter a rabble of Plebeians, with the Aediles.*

The people were assembled in the market place ready to disavow their choice of Coriolanus, but prepared—neither they nor the Tribunes—for no such business as this. So, called upon for help, they appear as a "rabble." It will be a very different matter when, for the later encounter, they have been "collected . . . by tribes" and drilled in the required behavior.

Secondly, while the plebeians are mustering to the support of their Tribunes, the direction to the Senators is

*They all bustle about Coriolanus.*

It is one of the play's characteristically descriptive stage directions; and it suggests a certain embarrassment and fuss, the Senators little less perturbed than the Tribunes are.

> You are at point to lose your liberties:
> Marcius would have all from you; Marcius,
> Whom late you have named for Consul.

And to the shocked reproach from the Senate side that

> This is the way to kindle, not to quench.
> To unbuild the city and to lay all flat.

he launches at Marcius, who would throw the popular power "in the dust," the tit-for-tat

> What is the city but the people?

with its powerful chorus of popular response:

> > True,
> The people are the city.

And thus can the political pendulum swing once it is started swinging.

For the Tribunes, cooler now and confident with their followers ranged behind them, this is a chance not to be missed, of pushing their power to its utmost. It marks them and their kind that they cannot resist the temptation. Their enemy, attacking them, has rashly talked treason too; and, says Sicinius:

> This deserves death.

Brutus adds categorically,

> Or let us stand to our authority
> Or let us lose it. We do here pronounce
> Upon the part o' the people, in whose power
> We were elected theirs, Marcius is worthy
> Of present death.

And, without more ado, the sentence ends, he is to be flung from the Tarpeian rock. Menenius—violence imminent, his side outnumbered—beseeches lenity. Marcius, silent till now, simply draws his sword, and says,

> No, I'll die here.

He adds, more sportingly,

> There's some among you have beheld me fighting:
> Come, try upon yourselves what you have seen me.

Urged by the Tribunes, they tumultuously do; and

*In this mutiny, the Tribunes, the Aediles, and the People,
are beat in.*

—as, with Marcius at the head of even a handful of men of good
fighting quality (Cominius is there, and Titus Lartius), such a
rabble might look to be.

But it is to be noted how the impromptu victory is taken:
Menenius' first thought is for Marcius to profit from it by
retreating to his house and leaving the reasonable rest of them to
patch up the best peace they can. One or two are left fighting
keen.[84] But

> Shall it be put to that?

—Romans at war with Romans—

> The gods forbid!

In affection for his hero the old man mitigates the effect of
Marcius' grimly vaunting

> On fair ground
> I could beat forty of them.

with the humor of his own

> I could myself
> Take up a brace o' the best of them; yea, the two Tribunes.

But it is a relief to have him gone.

Comment is practical:

> This man has marred his fortune.

—this is *not* the way to campaign for the consulship in Rome.[35]

~~~~~~~~~

[84] Cominius, apparently, one. But I fancy that the

> Stand fast:
> We have as many friends as enemies.

is misascribed to him. For if not, he changes his mind barely a moment later;
and, a little later still, a six-line speech conclusively puts him among the prudent
ones. Further, he and Coriolanus depart together.

[35] The Folio has marked an *exeunt* for Coriolanus and Cominius only; and the
minor speeches immediately following are given to *Patri*, translated by later
editors into First and Second Patrician, instead of to the Senators who have
fulfilled this need till now. One queries at first an (unrecorded) departure of the
Senators too; but at the end of the scene there still remains one Senator at least.
A possible explanation is that the Senators in their robes—whatever on
Shakespeare's stage these were—are meant to be withdrawn to the background,
the gathering to lose the last of its ceremonial aspect. This will add, by contrast,

And through Menenius' loyally laudatory

> His nature is too noble for the world:
> He would not flatter Neptune for his trident,
> Or Jove for 's power to thunder. . . .

can be heard, perhaps, the man of the world's sigh of exasperation
at being left to clear up if he can the mess this noble nature has
made of things. It issues in a final

> What the vengeance!
> Could he not speak 'em fair?

But a breathing-space at least has been gained, in which
Menenius himself can "speak 'em fair," can try, as he said,

> whether my old wit be in request
> with those that have but little . . .

and here we may recall our first sight of him at the play's
opening, and the skill with which he quieted the mutiny over the
corn. This is a harder task. Brutus and Sicinius are not to be so
cajoled. They possess authority, moreover, to which he takes care
to show deference, while Marcius has put himself indefensibly in
the wrong. And the people are for the moment—wherefore the
Tribunes are astutely demanding death without delay—authentically incensed against him, witness the full chorus of reiterated
"No, no . . ." which greets his mere tentative naming as "the
Consul Coriolanus." He must make for him, then, must Menenius,
such a place with the people as the Tribunes dare not, for shame—
will not, for policy—obstruct.

First, it is to a regard for Rome's good name:

> whose gratitude
> Towards her deserved children is enrolled
> In Jove's own book . . .

Then:

> What has he done to Rome that's worthy death?
> Killing our enemies, the blood he hath lost—
> Which, I dare vouch, is more than that he hath,
> By many an ounce—he dropped it for his country;

to the semblance of authority worn by Brutus and Sicinius, reappearing at the
head of their rabble.

And what is left, to lose it by his country
Were to us all, that do 't and suffer it,
A brand to the end o' the world.

"Were to us all"—they are one in citizenship with him, and all are Rome.

The Tribunes see that they must put a stop to this, must let loose the pent wrath of the people, before, under such soothing, it abates altogether. But—each minute a gain—Menenius begs for

One word more, one word.

And of full effect he makes it; with its warning whither "tiger-footed rage" may lead, his repicturing to the people of their soldier

bred i' the wars
Since he could draw a sword . . .

and his final promise to bring him back to them compliant in spirit. And the Senatorial

Noble Tribunes,
It is the humane way. . . .

solidly supports him.

They are practiced politicians, are the Tribunes, and can quickly tack and veer, and turn moderation to account as well as rage. If they do not now give Marcius another chance, they may well, under the effect of such appeals for him, split their own party. If they do, and he does not take it, he will probably split his own, and they will have him the more at their mercy. Besides, Menenius will almost certainly fail to bring him tamely to heel. So Sicinius generously consents; a touch of sardonic humor in his

Noble Menenius,
Be you, then, as the people's officer . . .

And the

Masters, lay down your weapons.
Go not home.
Meet on the market place. . . .

is but a menace postponed. To Menenius and the Senators, indeed, Sicinius is coldly explicit:

Where, if you bring not Marcius we'll proceed
In our first way.

Menenius' "old wit" has won him somewhat; but despite the jovially confident

> I'll bring him to you.

he knows how precariously little yet. And the scene ends upon the ominous muted note of his

>                     He must come,
> Or what is worst will follow.

as he and the Senators depart to fulfill the no easier second half of their task—if they can!

Coriolanus absent, and his violent stimulus to the action lacking, its pulse has kept a steadier beat. There is no slackening, the tension is sustained; and we are stirred to question: will he once more yield to persuasion, or no?

### VOLUMNIA'S SHARE IN THE QUARREL

Finding him at his house, the young nobility around him, high-mettled and willful as he, truly it does not seem likely.[86] He is at the highest pitch of indignant wrath:

> Let them pull all about mine ears; present me
> Death on the wheel, or at wild horses' heels;
> Or pile ten hills on the Tarpeian rock
> That the precipitation might down stretch
> Below the beam of sight; yet will I still
> Be thus to them.

flattered in it by these young supporters of his own breed and mind whom conflict begins to gather to him—one of them exclaiming,

>          You do the nobler.

[86] The Folio's stage direction speaks here only of his entering *with Nobles*; actually it is later, on his way to banishment, that he is said to be accompanied to the city gate by *the young Nobility of Rome*. But the distinction implied at both points between them (whether called *Nobles* or *young Nobility*) and the rest of his party is the same, and its meaning is, I think, clear. At first he has, of course, the Senate on his side; and among the variously termed Patricians, Gentry, Nobles, some will be Senators, some not. Step by step, in his intransigence, he alienates the Senators, and—if it can be shown, if the theater company can muster sufficient numbers—possibly some of the elders among the mere gentry too. But the young nobility—men more or less of his own age—side with him to the last. And it is at this point in the action that—though not much is made of it—they begin to be distinguished from the rest.

—pricked the more to it by a most unexpected crossing just encountered:

> I muse my mother
> Does not approve me further. . . .

We may note how Shakespeare here concentrates his action, dovetails it, coils it like a spring to give it strength. Marcius left the Capitol with Cominius, who has now, apparently, gone elsewhere; we shall learn where and why later. He himself has been at home long enough for a first encounter with Volumnia, the result of it shown in the outburst with which the scene opens, the violent recoil from her sober counsel; and that this *is* the result of it to be surmised from the sight of her as she slowly follows him and stands, disapproval in her attitude, until he turns to discover and ask,

> Why did you wish me milder?[37]

Here too the depicting of Marcius takes a more intimate turn. Man of action, of impulse, and of quick response to his fellows whether in anger or affection, we do not find him reflecting in solitude. Shakespeare allots him but one short soliloquy, and that to mark his loneliness and defeat.[38] He is brought nearest to consciousness of himself—the boyish self-consciousness that plagues him a very different thing!—when he looks, as now, in the glass of his mother's opinion of him. This has been satisfyingly flattering so far; he "muses" the more that she should now wish him to be false to himself. And the tragedy of character gains shape.

He yielded to persuasion and was false to himself when he put on the gown of humility and stood begging for votes in the market place. But at least he did it ill; and he atoned to himself, moreover, when the chance came, by giving Tribunes and people a fuller taste of his true mind than otherwise he would have done —gave it to his own prejudice too. This new temptation to go back upon himself finds him at first more violent in resistance, yet the less able to resist.

---

[37] A simple effect, lost in the modern editorial delaying of her entrance by nine lines.

[38] The exclamatory "Better it is to die, better to starve . . ." in the scene in the market place is hardly a soliloquy.

Having vented in defiance his astonishment that Volumnia should so rebuke him, he listens to her respectfully, lovingly; to Menenius and the Senators, coming in hope and doubt from their parley with the Tribunes; to Cominius, who later reports from the market place that the issue must be faced—to all their politic advice. But it is a chilling change from his mother's accustomed fervors to the biting

> You might have been enough the man you are
> With striving less to be so. . . .

apt and deserved though this may be. That he is right in what he has said, but that he should wait, should he, to say it until those that hold him wrong are in his power?—it is foxy doctrine. He has been, protests genial old Menenius, "too rough, something too rough. . . ." From Volumnia, again, who claims for herself

> a brain that leads my use of anger
> To better vantage.

(not that, tested so little later, this appears) he faces a

> You are too absolute.

He, then, their hero, if he is to be their Consul, has some most unheroic lessons to learn. To return to the Tribunes and publicly repent what he has spoken—which he would not do to the gods! But he listens still. He has no taste for argument. Strange that it should be his mother cleverly proving to him, his friends applauding, that a lie told to his fellow Romans here to gain his ends no more dishonors him than it would in war thus

> to take in a town with gentle words,
> Which else would put you to your fortune and
> The hazard of much blood . . .

But a good argument doubtless. Not a very admirable picture, though, that she sketches of him for his copying:

> with this bonnet in thy hand . . .
> Thy knee bussing the stones—for in such business
> Action is eloquence, and the eyes of the ignorant
> More learned than the ears—waving thy head,
> (Which often) thus correcting thy stout heart,
> Now humble as the ripest mulberry
> That will not hold the handling. . . .

And, even more than in his donning of the gown of humility,
does it put him to a part which, he protests, he never can
"discharge to the life." But, waging this sort of war, his friends
have him at their mercy as never had his enemies when he faced
*them* sword in hand. For his wife's sake, his son's, in the Senators'
cause and the nobles', it is his duty, so it seems, to forswear himself. And Volumnia, argument unavailing, coaxes and chides
him like a child, and, as a last resource, treats him to a hot fit of
the very temper she has so disastrously bred in him.

He is swung from a baited

> Well, I must do 't.

and from his own yet sorrier filling-in of her sorry picture of
him—

> Away, my disposition, and possess me
> Some harlot's spirit! my throat of war be turned,
> Which quired with my drum, into a pipe
> Small as an eunuch . . .
> a beggar's tongue
> Make motion through my lips, and my armed knees,
> Who bowed but in my stirrup, bend like his
> That hath received an alms! . . .

—to the violent revolt of

> I will *not* do 't
> Lest I surcease to honour mine own truth,
> And by my body's action teach my mind
> A most inherent baseness.

but, finally, as she rounds on him, to a boylike

> Pray, be content,
> Mother, I am going to the market place;
> Chide me no more. . . .

It is the endearing side of him.

> I'll mountebank their loves,
> Cog their hearts from them, and come home beloved
> Of all the trades in Rome. Look, I am going:
> Commend me to my wife. . . .

The invincible soldier! Vulnerable in the simplicity of his
affections, as son, husband, father, friend! Pure patriot, by his

unquestioning lights; his life his country's! As a politician, a fool!

He is foredoomed to fail in this coming test, with which the long strain of his campaign for the consulship is to end. It does not lie in him to be cynically false to his nature. He knows only how to be true even to its faults. Still, he will please them if he can; to have his mother turn her back on him in anger distresses him. So, with "Mildly" for his watchword—a wry irony evolving from the sound of it as he and Menenius pass it between them— he sets out again at the head of his party.

## BANISHMENT

Sicinius and Brutus (the appointment was for the market place; when we see them enter, then, we shall presume them there) have not wasted time. While Senators and nobles have been at odds with their candidate and leader, they, by contrast, have been drilling their followers and developing their tactics. Coriolanus can still be best accused of aiming at tyrannical power; and, says Brutus,

> In this point charge him home. . . .

But "if he evade us there. . . ," if, that is to say, Menenius has succeeded in making him see reason, why, to tax him with having, in his hatred for the people, deprived them of their share of the spoil "got on the Antiates," will certainly rouse his wrath again. He is coming, they hear: accompanied, of course, by old Menenius

> and those Senators
> That always favoured him.

There are others, then; and his party can be divided. Then come their last-minute instructions to the Aedile. The people have been organized in their legal groups? Good. Let them listen for their leaders' voices; and, says Sicinius,

> when they hear me say "It shall be so
> I' the right and strength o' the Commons," be it either
> For death, for fine, or banishment, then let them
> If I say fine, cry "fine," if death, cry "death". . . .

—for only with such docile followers can a democratic leader do himself full credit, reap the moment's maximum harvest. But there are, besides, the opposite uses to which a crowd can be put:

> And when such time they have begun to cry,
> Let them not cease, but with a din confused
> Enforce the present execution. . . .

Then Brutus, kindling to the opportunity:

> Put him to choler straight.

and the rest will follow. The unhappy Coriolanus is no better than a child in their hands. Sicinius, beneath the surface, is as excited:

> Well, here he comes.

It is a tense and a pregnant moment.

Menenius, on the way here, has been harping, seemingly, on the single string, its note varied only from the parting "Mildly" to this

> Calmly, I do beseech you.

—Marcius' muttered answer not reassuring! The opponents face each other like duelists with a ceremonious salute; and what could be more exemplary than Marcius'

> The honoured gods
> Keep Rome in safety, and the chairs of justice
> Supplied with worthy men! plant love among's!
> Throng our large temples with the shows of peace,
> And not our streets with war!

Menenius applauds, as might a proud tutor his pupil:

> A noble wish!

The Tribunes duly proceed:

> Draw near, ye people.

And the Aedile sustains their dignity:

> List to your Tribunes! Audience! Peace, I say!

Now comes maneuvering for position. Is this to be the end of the dispute? Marcius demands; Sicinius in turn:

> If you submit you to the people's voices,
> Allow their officers, and are content
> To suffer lawful censure for such faults
> As shall be proved upon you?

"Submit . . . censure . . . faults . . ."; it is a bitter pill. The Tribunes hope, the Senators fear, that he will never swallow it. With a Spartan

> I am content.

he does. Upon which, his friends cannot in prudence but see, the business had best be brought to a quick finish. Yet Menenius, though he himself sees it—

> Lo! citizens, he says he is content. . . .

—cannot resist pleading once more the cause that is already won, so well has he pleaded it; the advocate's common fault! "Warlike service" and "wounds" must again be commended; and Marcius himself, as before, must mock-modestly protest,

> Scratches with briers;
> Scars to move laughter only.

And the fresh tribute to his soldiership stirs him, despite Cominius' caution, to reopen the quarrel:

> What is the matter
> That being passed for Consul with full voice,
> I am so dishonoured that the very hour
> You take it off again?

—then he sees his error, and checks himself. But, if the Tribunes have failed so far to "put him to choler," they will not now:

> We charge you, that you have contrived to take
> From Rome all seasoned office, and to wind
> Yourself into a power tyrannical;
> For which you are a traitor to the people.

A two-edged thrust!

> The fires i' the lowest hell fold in the people!
> Call me *their* traitor! . . .

—no holding him after that!

   The people are ahead of their leaders here. Spontaneously the cry rises:

> To the rock, to the rock with him!

So now the supple demagogue can play the moderate man, gain credit with the moderate men of the other side, and insure himself

against reaction, should that come. The people are right. Marcius'
treachery to them

> Deserves the extremest death. . . .
> But since he hath
> Served well for Rome—

(Brutus is more than a little patronizing) sentence on him
shall mercifully be commuted to banishment for life. Neither
Menenius' comically frantic

> Is this the promise that you made your mother?

nor Cominius' noble plea, can turn Coriolanus from his defiant
wrath, the Tribunes from their triumph. And in their lessoned
unison the people echo once and again:

> It shall be so! It shall be so!
> Let him away!
> He's banished, and it shall be so.

Against such a chorus the single voice sounds nobly:

> You common cry of curs! whose breath I hate
> As reek o' the rotten fens, whose love I prize
> As the dead carcasses of unburied men
> That do corrupt my air . . .

and the superlative pride is warranted of the

> I banish you.

To his grim presage of what must be in store for such a mob
and for their Rome the Tribunes listen in complacent silence, the
people heedlessly, awaiting but the sight of his departure—

> Despising,
> For you, the city, thus I turn my back:
> There is a world elsewhere.[39]

~~~~~~

[39] It is just possible, I think, that F's quaintly corrupted stage direction:
*Exeunt Coriolanus, Cominius, with Cumaligs* (due to a muddled deletion in the
MS evidently) has to do with the several other stage directions and hints in
the text meant to indicate the growing division among Coriolanus' supporters (see
p. 229, note 36, and page 239, note 40). Was the *with* to have been followed
by particulars of those that accompanied him and those that did not, and did
Shakespeare, for lack of room or any other likely reason, content himself rather
with the *cum aliis*, leaving the fact that some went one way, some another to be
deduced (and implemented by the actors) from the opening stage direction of
the next scene: *Enter Coriolanus . . . with the young Nobility of Rome*; the

—to take their time once more from the fugleman-Aedile with a
jubilant

> Our enemy is banished! He is gone! Hoo! hoo!

though its ending is mere wolfish clamor.

"Despising, for you, the city . . ."; there is the first faint sound—
if the actor can accent it, and we are quick to hear—of the
deeper and more tragic discord to come.

Brutus and Sicinius meanwhile will lose nothing of a popular
triumph, nor of their revenge. The hero, cheered but a few hours
since, shall now be hooted through those same streets:

> Go, see him out at gates, and follow him,
> As he hath followed you, with all despite;
> Give him deserved vexation. . . .

—it is the mob's part. For the assertion of their own inflated
dignity:

> Let a guard
> Attend us through the city.


## THE DEPARTURE

Marcius is at once more likable in adversity than in triumph.
Of the cheering crowds that greeted, so short a while back, his
conqueror's entry, of the gathered Senate praising and honoring
him, out of all Rome nothing friendly seems left him as he takes
his way to exile, but his mother, his wife, two tried friends, and
this silent, useless handful of the young nobility, reluctant though
they are to see their hero depart; and these he will leave behind.
But he makes no complaint, has no word against the Tribunes—
in that omission the perfectest contempt!—and, for the people,
only the humorously bitter

> the beast
> With many heads butts me away.

He can rally his mother's spirits by retorting on her a choice few
of the precepts with which she was wont to load him, and with
a bantering

elders, but for Cominius and Menenius, having definitely deserted him? Mere
conjecture, and the point a small one; but the very smallest may have its worth
in a reconstructing of the play's intended staging.

What, what, what!

when anger breaks from her—

> Now the red pestilence strike all trades in Rome
> And occupations perish!

even as his own, to her reproving, was so apt to do. His harsher

> Nay, I prithee, woman!

vented upon his wife, is rather curb to himself lest he give way to grief as she is doing. Menenius—

> Thou old and true Menenius . . .

—already in tears, he comforts with kindly affection. Cominius, of sterner mettle, he calls on to

> tell these sad women
> 'Tis fond to wail inevitable strokes
> As 'tis to laugh at them.

To the wreck of his own fortunes there is no more reference than the boyishly simple

> I'll do well yet.

But this is the Marcius passingly glimpsed, who remembered, amid the acclaiming shouts, the poor man in Corioles who had once used him kindly, and, after victory, the widows there, and the "mothers that lack sons."

But beneath the cheerful courage, the buoyancy of

> I shall be loved when I am lacked.

we become conscious of a dark, of a sinister sorrow, its shadow apparent in the

> I go alone,
> Like to a lonely dragon, that his fen
> Makes feared and talked of more than seen. . . .

of a suffering repressed, but up-welling in that single

> O, the gods!

He will go to his exile alone, as befits his pride; and whatever they hear of him it shall be

> never of me aught
> But what is like me formerly.

No regrets, therefore, no compunction! He is the same Marcius still; and what cannot soften will but harden him the more.[40]

## THOSE LEFT BEHIND

Brutus and Sicinius follow at his heels, the Aedile attending them. Their amiable plan to have a mob hoot him "out at gates" is thwarted. He has gone. The sooner, therefore, their violence having served its turn, the people are quieted and sent home the better. This is the Aedile's task. Besides, a change of policy is called for now.

> The nobility are vexed. . . .

—and doubtless will repent their weakness in letting Coriolanus go.[41] Therefore, says the sagacious Brutus,

> Now we have shown our power
> Let us seem humbler after it is done
> Than when it was a-doing.

Neither do they fancy an encounter with Volumnia as she now returns—a lowering thundercloud!—with Virgilia and Menenius from the farewell at the gate. But they dodge unavailingly. For the cruel strain of that parting asks fuller relief than in tears—and here they are, very much to the purpose.

Marcius has gone, ominously self-controlled, to nurse his

---

[40] The young nobility, "my friends of noble touch," here also left behind, are evidently closely related to the "three or foure of his friends only" who, in North's Plutarch, did accompany him. The main point of the change is, of course, to bring Marcius, without more complication, to Antium all alone. A lesser dramatist might, then, have rid himself of the young nobility altogether. But to Shakespeare the enrichment of Marcius' character, slight as it is, by his dismissal of them at the gate, is worth while. And it costs him but half a line of text.

[41] It is likely, I should say, that the sight of the young nobility returning from their farewell to Coriolanus at the city gate (to be followed in a minute by Volumnia, Virgilia and Menenius) and their demeanor when they see the Tribunes suggests this

> The nobility are vexed. . . .

to Sicinius. They would merely cross the stage. Cominius would presumably be with them. There is nothing, of course, either in text or stage direction to indicate this; but it fits with the rest of the scene's business. Clearly they should have appeared to follow Marcius to the gate, for he has said to them

> *when I am forth,*
> Bid me farewell, and smile.

wrongs and breed them into—we shall see what monstrous shape.
With Menenius what's done is done. Why waste more words on
the fellows? So he finds himself pleading to Volumnia—and as
fruitlessly as to her son. For the touch of the unexpected with
which Shakespeare is wont to reinforce such eddies in the action
as this: Virgilia too, foregoing her "gracious silence," sets about
Sicinius, seconds Volumnia valiantly. The wretched Tribunes
take refuge from the volleying words, at first in scandalized
astonishment:

> Are you mankind? . . . O blessed heavens!

then in cant; their answer to Volumnia's

> I would my son
> Were in Arabia, and thy tribe before him,
> His good sword in his hand.

to Virgilia's

> He 'ld make an end of thy posterity.

to Volumnia's

> Bastards and all!
> Good man, the wounds that he does bear for Rome!

a smooth, white-of-the-eye,

> I would he had continued to his country
> As he began, and not unknit himself
> The noble knot he made.
> I would he had.

To which her retort comes plumply:

> "I would he had!" 'Twas you incensed the rabble:
> Cats . . .

Only a dignified departure is left them:

> Pray, let us go.

appropriately tinged with malice:

> Why stay we to be baited
> With one that wants her wits?

They gone, and the storm past, he trusts, Menenius essays for
solace:

> You have told them home;
> And, by my troth, you have cause. You'll sup with me?

—old age's comfort in the commonplace! Virgilia, spent by unwonted wrath, is in tears again. But Volumnia:

> Anger's my meat; I sup upon myself,
> And so shall starve with feeding. Come, let's go:
> Leave this faint puling and lament as I do.
> In anger, Juno-like. . . .

These are the natures—like mother, like son—to be broken, never bent; born to catastrophe.

### TRADERS IN THE IGNOBLE

*Enter a Roman and a Volsce.*

Before we see the noble and heroic fallen, infatuate, into infamy, Marcius, amazingly, a traitor to his country, we are given—for edification!—this marginal passage of cheerful trading in the ignoble. The Roman is a Fifth Column fighter, a Volscian spy, on his way to his masters to tell them that, Coriolanus banished, now is the time for them to take their revenge on Rome. His name, it appears, is Nicanor. He luckily encounters a Volscian comrade, one Adrian, who, being in something the same line of business, has been sent to discover him in Rome. He knows Adrian at once, who does not recognize him in his present guise—or disguise:

> You had more beard when I last saw you. . . .

his quizzical apology. The Roman bringing good news, the couple warm to each other:

> the nobles receive so to heart the banishment of that worthy Coriolanus, that they are in a ripe aptness to take all power from the people, and to pluck from them their Tribunes for ever. . . .

—which is not true, we shall learn later; but no matter, since it is good news, not necessarily the truth, that curries favor for your Nicanors.

> I shall, between this and supper, tell you most strange things from Rome, all tending to the good of their adversaries. . . .

continues this pleasant specimen of them, preening himself on the sensation he will make. Coriolanus banished, Aufidius and his Volscians ready to strike:

I am joyful to hear of their readiness, and am the man, I think, that shall set them in present action. So, sir, heartily well met, and most glad of your company.

And renegade Roman and Volscian go their way together, arm in arm, and as merry as grigs.

The scene forms a bridge between Coriolanus' departure from Rome and his appearance in Antium, suggests some likely period of time passing between the two. Also it shows us a seamier side to the magnificent and tragic treason he is about to commit. He will at least not draw sordid profit from it, and be merry over it.

## ANTIUM

*Enter Coriolanus, in mean apparel, disguised and muffled.*

From now to its end the tone of the play is changed. Marcius is changed, or rather—since men do not change—he seems no longer himself. The vengeance incarnate he becomes is but an empty simulacrum of himself; "a kind of nothing," Cominius calls him later. His troubles until now have come upon him because he could not learn to be false to his proudly faulty nature. But he has at least been honestly himself in struggling with them —and with the tricky Tribunes—however faultily. Now, under defeat, his untried soul will abjure the spontaneous loyalty, the faith, that had chiefly made him what he was; and he will be the mere tool of his vengeance, until, abjuring this, he is himself again. Meanwhile the passionate and unstable, temptation-tossed Aufidius will be covertly compassing his destruction. By such twisted and blind paths is it that the action now proceeds.

Marcius appears alone. It is the first such solitary appearance in the play, and will be the more striking because of that.[42] Till

---

[42] The first and the last for that matter, even as the scene thus begun contains the play's sole soliloquy. A play of action, not reflection; by its nature it does not run to soliloquies.

One may note, in passing, the baldness of the introductory

A goodly city is this Antium.

Shakespeare, in his maturity, is master of a dozen or more different ways of indirectly locating his scenes, as vaguely or as exactly as he may choose. But he will still use means as plain and direct as Sir Philip Sidney's notorious (and possibly apocryphal) placard, if they happen to be dramatically effective also.

now, too, we have seen him only either in fighting trim or in the panoply of his triumph and his consulship, except for the grotesque interlude of the *gown of humility*; his present *mean apparel* is a grimmer variation of it. Outcast, destitute, unarmed, in this city where—pride bitterly reminds him—discovery could mean death, he is seeking his chief enemy Aufidius.[43] And from a soliloquy—short, and the only one allotted to him—we learn why.

He is here to enlist with the Volscians against Rome. It has come to that with him. Neither now nor later are we told of any process of debate within him, any struggle or yielding to temptation. He simply comments now—coldly, cynically—upon the fact that such spiritual revolutions do occur, from hate to love, and love to hate; and

> So with me:
> My birth-place hate I, and my love's upon
> This enemy town.[44]

---

[43]      At Antium lives he? . . .
         I would I had a cause to seek him there. . . .
—the unconsciously ironic words, spoken at the very height of his good fortune, may well have lodged in our minds.

     Destitute, unarmed: Shakespeare does not stress the point of poverty, "my misery" covering much more than that, if that; but the "meanness" of his apparel, superfluous to mere disguise, seems meant loosely to suggest it. And it is evident that, in the encounter with Aufidius' servants, he at least wears no sword.

[44] The phrase
         Some trick not worth an egg . . .
recalls Hamlet's
         delicate and tender prince,
     Whose spirit with divine ambition puffed
     Makes mouths at the invisible event,
     Exposing what is mortal and unsure
     To all that fortune, death and danger dare,
     Even for an egg-shell . . .
It is not to say that there was, as he wrote, any constructive connection between the two in Shakespeare's mind, but the parallel is there; between Fortinbras the happy and Coriolanus the unhappy man of action, the one that (says Hamlet enviously) is ready
         greatly to find quarrel in a straw,
     When honour's at the stake . . .
his sense of honor exalting him, the other coming to see men and friends
         On a dissension of a doit, break out
         To bitterest enmity . . .
while his extravagant sense of his honorable duty to himself only betrays him to deep dishonor.

But it is of a piece with the rest of him that there should have
been no such debate or struggle. Of the faculty of introspection
he most certainly has none. Not once do we hear him question
himself. He acts upon conviction, and is never less than fully
convinced. That has helped to make him a fine fighter. Moreover,
he must act; inaction is against nature with him, and exile has
condemned him to it. And in what he does there will be no
compromise, no middle course taken. His soldier's genius and his
love of country have inspired him to the doing of great deeds,
and the thwarting of these forces in him deprives him of all
purpose in life. It is no argument that has turned him traitor.
But the present sight of him—so altered and worn that Aufidius,
who has five times fought him foot to foot, does not know him—
speaks eloquently enough of the lonely misery endured, until, in
some dark moment, natural love dead in him, he sought salvation
in hate.

Of this sight of him so altered Shakespeare makes much.
Deferential enquiry for "great Aufidius'" house takes him to its
hall-fire, to stand there, a gaunt, muffled, forbidding figure, while,
contrastingly, cheerful music plays within and the liveried
servants pass to and fro on the business of the feast. Ironically
submissive to his first rebuff,

> I have deserved no better entertainment,
> In being Coriolanus.

it is the old Marcius that answers with an ominous

> Away!

to the temerity of the Second Servant coming to oust him. What
to make of him and that humbly dignified

> Let me but stand; I will not hurt your hearth.

A third servant, with the first two to back him, will deal with the
fellow:

> What are you?
> A gentleman.
> A marvellous poor one!
> True, so I am.

But another rash move to oust him brings the Third Servant
within reach of that formidable arm, to be sent spinning by a

touch from it. These are matters for their master. But awaiting
Aufidius, the Third Servant holds his jack-in-office course:

> Where dwell'st thou?
> Under the canopy.
> Under the canopy?
> Ay.
> Where's that?
> I' the city of kites and crows.

while Marcius, the fateful moment nearing, finds a sardonically
trivial satisfaction in mystifying these blockheads, a solider one
when, turning on the unlucky Third Servant with a

> Thou prat'st; serve with thy trencher: hence!

he whacks him over the head with it.

Aufidius appears; he also, in his feasting finery, little like the
man we saw last, bloody with his wounds, savagely sullen in
defeat. Genial, flushed with wine, he surveys the uncouth
stranger. He has drunk enough to allow for an obstinate repeating
of

> What's thy name?

a petulantly willful

> I know thee not.

while the haggard gaze is leveled at him. And when at last the
steeled voice says,

> My name is Caius Marcius. . . .

he sobers to very dumbness, listens at first stupent. Nor is
Marcius, nor are we, to know until the whole tale has been
rigorously told, how he will take it, what he will do.

Marcius is as absolute as ever, and as proud, still prouder in
ill fortune than in good. He does not excuse, nor condescend to
justify, nor find fine phrases for what he is ready to do; "in
mere spite" to fight against his "thankless country," his

> cankered country, with the spleen
> Of all the under fiends . . .

and with as fierce a hate for the "dastard nobles," his own party,
who have suffered him

> by the voice of slaves to be
> Hooped out of Rome.

as for the slaves themselves.

He stoops to no flattery of Aufidius, pretends to no more thought for him and his Volscians than as mere instruments of revenge. A callous bargain; scornfully provokes Aufidius if he will not strike it:

> if so be
> Thou dar'st not this, and that to prove more fortunes
> Thou'rt tired, then, in a word, I also am
> Longer to live most weary, and present
> My throat to thee and to thy ancient malice,
> Which not to cut would show thee but a fool. . . .

Not in mercy then, but as callously, and to his own profit and content, let Aufidius end an enemy's misery here and now. This, in Marcius, is no bravado, but a sober measuring of the worth of revenge to him. He clinches his argument—

> Since I have ever followed thee with hate,
> Drawn tons of blood out of thy country's breast,
> And cannot live but to thy shame, unless
> It be to do thee service.

—and awaits, as uncertain as are we, the issue.

Aufidius, come to credit eyes and ears, has heard dumbfounded these amazing things unfolding, while within him one responsive impulse ousts another; until at last:

> O, Marcius, Marcius!
> Each word thou hast spoke hath weeded from my heart
> A root of ancient envy. . . .

—the generous emotion gushes forth, playing like a warm stream upon the ice, this ice that is Marcius. But he, for his part, yields, nevertheless, with little grace to the rhapsodies and embraces of his so suddenly converted foe, nor responds at all to such flowery rhetoric as the

> Know thou first,
> I loved the maid I married; never man
> Sighed truer breath; but that I see thee here,
> Thou noble thing, more dances my rapt heart
> Than when I first my wedded mistress saw
> Bestride my threshold. Why, thou Mars! . . .

Only when he hears of the "power on foot," of the Volscian plan
already made for

> pouring war
> Into the bowels of ungrateful Rome . . .

does he tardily, sternly, utter that

> You bless me, gods!

—and the thankfulness must sound strange in his own ears. For
the rest: the leadership proffered, the welcome from the "friendly
Senators" awaiting him, Aufidius' superlative

> A thousand welcomes!
> And more a friend than e'er an enemy . . .

—he accepts it all in silence, passing in to the feast, little like a man
so lavishly granted his desire. He goes—already—as to his doom.[45]

Withdrawn to a respectful distance, First and Second Servant
have been listening prick-eared:

> Here's a strange alteration!

------

[45] "Such flowery rhetoric": to Marcius, at any rate, in such a mood as he is, it
will seem so. The contrast between the dry, angular phrasing of his speech to
Aufidius and the rich, decorative and flowing melody of Aufidius' response is
marked. A distinguished critic has connected—and somewhat carpingly—the dry
angularity with the fact that Shakespeare took entire phrases for the speech from
North's Plutarch, and used them unaltered. But this effect of a man speaking not
spontaneously, as Aufidius does, but after long and bitter brooding with painful
thought given to what he should say, speaking moreover not out of the fullness
but the very emptiness of his heart, is, I suggest, precisely the effect meant to
be made. And if Shakespeare found he could best make it by tacking together
phrases from Plutarch he would certainly do so.

Marcius, at the thrilling moment of joining forces with Cominius on the
battlefield before Corioles, had launched into something the same imagery that
Aufidius uses now. But he was happily himself then as he will never be again.
And, even so, that

> O, let me clip you
> In arms as sound as when I wooed, in heart
> As merry as when our nuptial day was done,
> And tapers turned to bedward.

denoted a harder temper than sounds from Aufidius'

> never man
> Sighed truer breath; but that I see thee here,
> Thou noble thing, more dances my rapt heart . . .

Shakespeare, in writing them, may or may not have had the likeness between the
two passages in mind. It is unlikely that an audience will remark it.

—and readily do they adapt their artlessly servile minds to it. A great man; they might have known that, of course, despite his rags, from his high-minded way with them. And if great, if, in the next breath "the rarest man i' the world," why, another must be the lesser. Promptly begins the comically pitiful little shuffle of loyalties, their servile version of the tragic treason upon which they have been eavesdropping.

> a greater soldier than he, you wot on.
> Who? my master?
> Nay, it's no matter for that.
> Worth six on him? Nay, not so neither: but I take him to be the better soldier.
> Faith, look you, one cannot tell how to say that. . . .

—for in prudence we must both commit ourselves, or neither. And to Third Servant strutting excitedly in—happy to have been knocked over the pate with his own trencher by so great a man— and to his reckless

> here's he that was wont to thwack our general. . . .

First Servant makes shocked protest:

> Why do you say "thwack our general"?

reducing him to double-quick recanting:

> I do not say "thwack our general. . . ."

But, with a wink and a wag of the head from Second Servant,

> Come, we are fellows and friends. . . .

the three are in a tale together.

The consummation of Coriolanus' welcome, the sight of him

> set at upper end o' the table; no question asked him by any of the Senators, but they stand bald before him. . . .

while

> Our general himself makes a mistress of him; sanctifies himself with's hand, and turns up the white o' the eye to his discourse. . . .

—this we see through the simpleton eyes of Third Servant, puffed with the pride of coming fresh from the very sight of it. The comic coloring of the picture heightens, by irony of contrast, its

tragic import. The blundering parroting of the talk at table over
the noble renegade's prospects—

> for, look you, sir, he has as many friends as enemies; which
> friends, sir, as it were, durst not, look you, sir, show themselves,
> as we term it, his friends, whilst he's in directitude. . . . But
> when they shall see, sir, his crest up again, and the man in blood,
> they will out of their burrows like conies after rain, and revel
> all with him.

—embellishes its cynical shrewdness. And already, while Aufidius
is still erecting his fragile fane of devotion to his late enemy, this
belittling of him by these faithful followers is providing for its
wreck.

The scene ends with a noncombatants' chorus in praise of war,
coming from Volscians too, who have just been soundly beaten
and accorded by their conquerors a merciful peace.


### ROME ONCE MORE

The Tribunes Sicinius and Brutus reappear; we are in Rome
again. They are pluming themselves upon

> the present peace
> And quietness o' the people . . .

upon—at this most appropriate moment!—having heard no more
of Coriolanus, while

> Here do we make his friends
> Blush that the world goes well, who rather had,
> Though they themselves did suffer by 't, behold
> Dissentious numbers pestering streets than see
> Our tradesmen singing in their shops and going
> About their functions friendly.

It may be so. But there are men—politicians and others—who
learn, whether by experience or from the book of their own natures, to think the worst of everyone. Menenius, passing by, out-
faces their complacency—

> Your Coriolanus is not much missed
> But with his friends: the Commonwealth doth stand.
> And so would do, were he more angry at it.

—with a glum, blunt

> All's well, and might have been much better if
> He could have temporised.

After which they take the opportunity that offers of edifyingly patronizing a group of humbly grateful citizens—who beseech the gods preserve them, who for

> Ourselves, our wives and children, on our knees,
> Are bound to pray for you both.

to be unctuously repaid by a showering of

> Good den our neighbours.
> Good den to you all, good den to you all. . . .
> Live and thrive!
> Farewell, kind neighbours. . . .

with—a sting for Menenius!—a

> we wished Coriolanus
> Had loved you as we did.

It is for a beginning to the play's ending that we are given this passage of sharp contrast with its beginning; the genial bullying of the citizens by Menenius, their brutal rating by Marcius, here replaced by the soft smiles of their Tribunes—from which official fool's paradise they are very quickly to be expelled.

From its beginning to the moment of Marcius' banishment the play has abounded in physical action, in battles and rioting. From now to the verge of its concluding catastrophe we shall have only the increasing tension of the threat of his reprisals; then, suddenly, their frustration. The battle to be fought now is one of moral forces, culminating in the struggle between Marcius and Volumnia, in which, silently at the last, he accepts defeat. The two sections of the play stand in nearly every respect contrasted. The scene with Aufidius in Antium may be called a bridge between the two; that of Marcius' death is in the nature of an epilogue.

The drama of Coriolanus' approach to his revenge begins at a very zero point, that of Brutus' fatuous

> Rome
> Sits safe and still without him.

Promptly an Aedile appears, to convey, with due official dignity,

the news, brought by "a slave, whom we have put in prison . . ."
that

> the Volsces with two several powers
> Are entered in the Roman territories. . . .

For Menenius, it is Marcius' banishing that has brought them,
Aufidius, doubtless, at their head. For Brutus, such an unpleasant
thing simply "cannot be" and the slave must be whipped for
saying so. "Cannot?"; but it has been, thrice within Menenius'
memory. Sicinius is as blandly confident:

> Tell not me;
> I know this cannot be.

Whereupon

> *Enter a Messenger.*

Shakespeare gives a hundred lines more to the completing of
this scene of the Tribunes' discomfiture, and the whole is a
minor masterpiece of treatment. He employs the economical
convention of the Messenger, which gives drama the continuity
of narrative. But, to vary and enrich it, the story to be told is put
into four mouths instead of one, differing in temper and quality,
each supplementing or revising the other. The Aedile is un-
hurried and correct. He has taken order with the slave; he reports
the matter; his duty is done. The first Messenger is precipitate
and perturbed; wide-eyed. Is it to be believed, this rumor

> that Marcius,
> Joined with Aufidius, leads a power 'gainst Rome,
> And vows revenge . . .

Menenius, for a moment, is at one with the Tribunes in disbelief.
But the pendulum is swung violently back by the coming of a
second Messenger in all haste to ·summon the pair without
ceremony to the Senate, the ill news cumulated into worse:

> A fearful army, led by Caius Marcius,
> Associated with Aufidius, rages
> Upon our territories; and have already
> O'erborne their way, consumed with fire, and took
> What lay before them.

And, before they can take breath to protest, comes finally Cominius, not only to confirm it but, with grimly humorous satisfaction, to point them out as the culprits:

> O, you have made good work.

Trouble not to be mended by the whipping of a slave! The Tribunes are struck dumb.

Cominius does not spare them, keeps Menenius impatiently demanding his news while he loads them with terrors:

> You have holp to ravish your own daughters, and
> To melt the city leads upon your pates,
> To see your wives dishonoured to your noses—

and—this is the fruit of their rule in Rome—

> *Your* temples burned in their cement, and
> *Your* franchises, whereon you stood . . .

Menenius—his still incredulous

> If Marcius should be joined with Volscians—

extinguished by the sardonic acclaim of

> If!
> He is their god; he leads them like a thing
> Made by some other deity than Nature,
> That shapes man better; and they follow him
> Against us brats. . . .

—takes up the refrain too:

> You have made good work,
> You, and your apron men . . .
> You have made fair work!

until Brutus at last finds a meek and fearful tongue:

> But is this true, sir?

Satisfaction with the vengeance to fall on the Tribunes—capable themselves now of little but agonized grimaces—mingles in Cominius and Menenius with genuine alarm for Rome.[46] This is shot through with renewed pride in Marcius—one of themselves—

---

[46] Brutus and Sicinius are semi-comic characters, and the actors of them were, I think, expected to make their conspicuous silence here even more conspicuous by facial play.

and the power of his name, this again with the shameful memory that they, his friends, abandoned him.

> We loved him; but, like beasts
> And cowardly nobles, gave way unto your clusters,
> Who did hoot him out o' the city.

The theme of betrayal and self-betrayal permeates the play. Some "clusters" gathering round—

> *Enter a troop of Citizens.*

—Menenius can relieve his mind with a little of his old frank abuse of them. Echoing from past clashes,

> Now he's coming. . . .
>                        as many coxcombs
> As you threw caps up will he tumble down,
> And pay you for your voices. . . .

Cominius echoing him with a

> Ye're goodly things, you voices!

they leave the poor citizens to their pitiful excuses—

> That we did we did for the best; and though we willingly consented to his banishment, yet it was against our will.

—and the Tribunes, freed from their daunting presence, to the flattering futility of

> Go, masters, get you home, be not dismayed:
> These are a side that would be glad to have
> This true which they so seem to fear. . . .

Spiritless all, they go their several ways. Menenius and Cominius:

> Shall's to the Capitol?
> O, ay; what else!

The Second Citizen to the rest:

> But come, let's home.

Sicinius to his fellow:

> Pray, let's go.

While as to Brutus, his rueful

> Would half my wealth
> Would buy this for a lie!

reminds us, incidentally, that politics and the leadership of the poor can be made to pay.

## AUFIDIUS DISILLUSIONED;
## MARCIUS SCANNED

The scene between Aufidius and his Lieutenant prepares the play's final stroke without discounting this by telling us too clearly what it is to be. The impulsive generosity to a fallen enemy has soon burned out in him, and Aufidius, recovered from the experience and ready to treat Marcius as an enemy again, can estimate his virtues and failings the more fairly, even though he is now but the more set to "potch" at his prodigious rival by

> some way
> Or wrath or craft may get him.

For generosity repented has hardened him.

> I do not know what witchcraft's in him. . . .

says the Lieutenant. Well, Aufidius himself has been its victim, and, beside him, will doubtless be

> darkened in this action . . .

—which, however, since there's to be Volscian profit in it, must be carried through. It is only too true that

> All places yield to him ere he sits down;
> And the nobility of Rome are his;
> The Senators and Patricians love him too:
> The Tribunes are no soldiers, and their people
> Will be as rash in the repeal as hasty
> To expel him thence. I think he'll be to Rome
> As is the osprey to the fish, who takes it
> By sovereignty of nature. . . .

But—! Now follows the coldly, carefully, qualified verdict of second-rate success upon first-rate failure:

> First he was
> A noble servant to them, but he could not
> Carry his honours even. Whether 'twas pride . . .
> whether defect of judgment . . .
> or whether nature,

Not to be other than one thing . . .
          but one of these,
As he has spices of them all—not all,
For I dare so far free him—made him feared,
So hated, and so banished. . . .

Let the greatly gifted man remember, then, that

          So our virtues
Lie in the interpretation of the time. . . .

and, their turn served, are apt to be canceled out. It will be so
with Coriolanus:

One fire drives out one fire; one nail, one nail;
Rights by rights founder, strengths by strengths do fail.

Aufidius, nursing his plans, his last lethal stroke conceived, is
oracular:

When, Caius, Rome is thine,
Thou are poor'st of all; then shortly are thou mine.[47]

The scene allows incidentally for the time taken by Cominius'
intercessory visit to Coriolanus, now encamped before Rome. This
is over when the next opens, with the tension notably increased by
its failure.

### NEMESIS NEARS

*Enter Menenius, Cominius, Sicinius, Brutus, the two
Tribunes, with others.*

—*with others*, listeners and onlookers; a token of the general
anxiety.

Grave as they saw it to be, their enjoyment in saddling the

---

[47] Such now unusual phrases as "not moving from the casque to the cushion"
and "even with the same austerity and garb as he controlled the war" increase
for us the difficulty of following Aufidius' analysis of Coriolanus' virtues and
defects, its repeated "whether . . . s" making it already difficult enough. (The
trick of the speech, one notes, is much that of Hamlet's "So oft it chances in
particular men. . . .") And in quoting it here I have had, so as to isolate the
continuity of thought, to reduce it to an ugly skeleton. Then, when it comes to
the more general comments on success and failure, we meet with a corruption of
the text—"hath not a tomb so evident as a chair . . ."—which no one yet, as far
as I know, has been able satisfactorily to clarify. Altogether, it is a troublesome
speech to the modern actor; and Aufidius, as a whole, may be called a troublesome character in the acting. Shakespeare, it seems, found him interesting, but
would not afford space for his expansion. (Cf. p. 173.)

Tribunes with the blame for it was some sign that Cominius and
Menenius had not, despite all, thought the situation quite hope-
less, had underlyingly felt, rather, that even though they had
deserved Marcius' hate, "and therein showed like enemies," yet
they were the men to redeem it. But Cominius has been on his
mission since: and

> He would not seem to know me.

Once, indeed, he did call him by his name. But thereafter,

> Coriolanus
> He would not answer to, forbad all names;
> He was a kind of nothing, titleless,
> Till he had forged himself a name o' the fire
> Of burning Rome.

Plea following plea, none moved him, nor will; Cominius is
hopelessly sure of it.

Menenius, on the other hand, protesting that he never can
succeed if Cominius has failed—

> He called me father,
> But what o' that? . . .
> Nay, if he coyed
> To hear Cominius speak, I'll keep at home.

—is plainly "coying" himself, and only waiting to be pressed
harder to consent, in his turn, to go. He is cheerful enough still
to be mockingly reminding the now quite crestfallen Brutus and
Sicinius that they

> have made good work!
> A pair of Tribunes that have racked for Rome,
> To make coals cheap . . .

There is no spirit left in them. Sicinius, begging him to go, is
reduced to the pitiful

> if you refuse your aid
> In this so never-needed help, yet do not
> Upbraid's with our distress. . . .

An "instant army" will be all they can muster for Rome's
protection.[48] They fall to wheedling and flattering him. Even if

---

[48] It is implied in more than one passage that the Tribunes now rule Rome,
and Aufidius has just remarked of them that they "are no soldiers." Theirs is, in

he fails, Sicinius says:

> Yet your good will
> Must have that thanks from Rome, after the measure
> As you intended well.

—which puts him on his mettle. A final show of diffidence, for tribute to "good Cominius" and his failure, and he is the buoyant old Menenius still:

> He was not taken well; he had not dined.
> The veins unfilled, our blood is cold, and then
> We pout upon the morning, are unapt
> To give or to forgive; but when we have stuffed
> These pipes and these conveyances of our blood
> With wine and feeding, we have suppler souls
> Than in our priest-like fasts. . . .

—the imagery characteristically recalls our first hearing from him with the fable of the Belly and the Members—

> therefore I'll watch him
> Till he be dieted to my request,
> And then I'll set upon him.

And, cheerily confident, off he goes.

Cominius has listened in silence. He shakes his head, strikes the stern note again:

> He'll never hear him. . . .
> I tell you, he does sit in gold, his eye
> Red as 't would burn Rome, and his injury
> The gaoler to his pity. . . .

pictures and prepares us for the pitiless figure we are soon to see.

Then, to end the scene, the step beyond the next is forecast:

> So that all hope is vain,
> Unless his noble mother and his wife,
> Who, as I hear, mean to solicit him
> For mercy to his country. . . .

As the crisis nears the action is knit the closer, that our attention may be the more closely held.

~~~~~~~~~~~~~~~~~~~~~~~~~~~~~~~~~~~~~~~~~~

fact, what would be called today a "pacifist" government, quite unprepared for war.

## MENENIUS TRIES, AND FAILS

*Enter Menenius to the Watch or Guard.*

Yet another encounter between patrician and commoners, and a scene of ebb and flow of emotion and humor before—it will be a contrast—the powerfully sustained tension of the trial to come.

Menenius deploys his tact. He answers the sentry's sharp challenge with affable praise:

> You guard like men, 'tis well. . . .

asserts his own quality with accustomed ease:

> but, by your leave,
> I am an officer of state, and come
> To speak with Coriolanus.

—in vain. The sentries disappointingly deserve his praise.

> You may not pass, you must return. . . .
> You'll see your Rome embraced with fire before
> You'll speak with Coriolanus.

He tries the flattery of familiarity:

> Good my friends,
> If you have heard your general talk of Rome,
> And of his friends there, it is lots to blanks,
> My name hath touched your ears: it is Menenius.

is brought to vaunting his own with the great man—

> I tell thee, fellow,
> Thy general is my lover. . . .

—and, in euphemistic phrase, the unconscionable services he has done him:

> Therefore, fellow,
> I must have leave to pass.

Hectorings and wittiness alike get plain answer:

> Faith, sir, if you had told as many lies in his behalf as you
> have uttered words in your own, you should not pass here. . . .

But the old gentleman persists, to be given finally a sound and most disrespectful talking to:

> You are a Roman, are you?
> I am, as thy general is.

> Then you should hate Rome, as he does. Can you, when you
> have pushed out your gates the very defender of them . . . ?

Truly these Volscian sentries know their own minds and can
speak them; the dose no pleasanter to Menenius for its likeness
to his own recent medicining of the Tribunes. And if it is to
come to an issue between fretful dignity on one side and discipline
with cold steel to warrant it on the other—

> Sirrah, if thy captain knew I were here, he would use me with
> estimation.
> Come, my captain knows you not.
> I mean thy general.
> My general cares not for you. Back, I say, go: lest I let forth
> your half-pint of blood. Back; that's the utmost of your having:
> back.
> Nay, but fellow, fellow—!

At which moment Coriolanus and Aufidius pass.
   After a sharp, soldierly

> What's the matter?

Coriolanus waits in silence, fulfillment of Cominius' picture of
him. Menenius, tossed between emotions, lets the lightest first
possess him; tit-for-tat with impudent sentries will restore him his
confident good humor.

> Now, you companion . . . you shall perceive that a Jack
> guardant cannot office me from my son Coriolanus. . . .

He is himself again in the jaunty extravagance of

> guess but by my entertainment with him, if thou standest not
> i' the state of hanging, or of some death more long in spectator-
> ship, and crueller in suffering; behold now presently and swoon
> for what's to come upon thee.

It gives him time, too, in which to face this changed Marcius,
distant, mute, hostile, companioned there with Aufidius. But he
neither hesitates nor calculates. Eloquence overflows in affection
and tears:

> The glorious gods sit in hourly synod about thy particular
> prosperity, and love thee no worse than thy old father Menenius
> does! O my son! my son! thou art preparing fire for us: look
> thee, here's water to quench it. . . .

and, for a final fillip, into the familiar humor:

> The good gods assuage thy wrath, and turn the dregs of it
> upon this varlet here; this, who, like a block, hath denied my
> access to thee.

The one word of the answer, spanning the space between them—

> Away!

—falls like a blow. The old man staggers under it. Had he ears for
aught else he might note in the sequent

> Wife, mother, child, I know not. . . .

the flaw in the armor of which that too rigid figure is himself
aware, might even read in the strain of the

> Yet—for I loved thee—
> Take this along, I writ it for thy sake
> And would have sent it. . . .

in this letter with which he is dismissed, defense ready to crumble.
But pride, if not affection, is now too wounded for him to think
of aught else.

Coriolanus and Aufidius pass on their way:

> This man, Aufidius,
> Was my beloved in Rome; yet thou beholdst!

to which utterance of twisted, tortured pride Aufidius pays
sardonic tribute:

> You keep a constant temper.

But Menenius can take a blow gallantly still, and pay back
mockery with mockery. To the sentries' jubilant

> Now, sir, is your name Menenius?
> 'Tis a spell, you see, of much power. You know the way home
> again.
> Do you hear how we are shent for keeping your greatness
> back?
> What cause, do you think, I have to swoon?

he returns as good as he gets, and better:

> I neither care for the world, nor your general: for such things
> as you, I can scarce think there's any, y'are so slight. . . .

—but it is graver defiance than that—

> He that hath a will to die by himself, fears it not from
> another. Let your general do his worst. . . .

—no business of theirs though!

> For you, be that you are, long; and your misery increase with
> age! I say to you, as I was said to, Away!

They are left laughing; won, nevertheless, to the verdict of

> A noble fellow, I warrant him.

## VOLUMNIA COMES, AND THE CONQUEROR IS CONQUERED

Coriolanus and Aufidius were, it seems, on their way to a
council of war; they are taking their places at its table now.[49]
First, formally and for all to hear, the two exchange assurances
that so far in this strange business all has been frankly done.
Aufidius is most generous in his assurance. Coriolanus then falls
to confession; and—how changed!—it is of kindly, politic trick-
ery. "With a cracked heart" it was, then, that he stood outfacing
Menenius there; and he had offered him in the letter, to make
things easier for them both, something to carry away that he yet
knew must be rejected. It was only

> A very little
> I have yielded to. . . .

but it is right they know it. That is all finished now. Then

> *Shout within.*

He asks what it may mean, knowing too well:

> Shall I be tempted to infringe my vow
> In the same time 'tis made? . . .

The dreaded trial has come. He steels himself:

> I will not.

---

[49] The Folio stage direction for the first scene is simply *Enter Coriolanus and
Aufidius.* Capell added *and others*; and pretty plainly Coriolanus is not speaking
to Aufidius alone. The council of war at a table set upon the inner stage is as
easily deduced. The curtains will be closed as the two pass across the outer stage,
finding Menenius there. They could be discovered when the curtains are drawn,
the fifteen lines or so spoken by the Watch and Menenius allowing them that
much time to take their places, or, having gone off by the side door, they can
wait and enter again upon the inner stage.

The pending struggle has been fully prepared. Cominius, Consul and General, revered as both, kneeling, repulsed, the loved Menenius dismissed—this the one aspect, completed by the sentry's admiring view of the traitor-hero as

> the rock, the oak not to be wind-shaken.

For another; he has armored himself with an oath offered to Aufidius, a vow solemnly taken. The closer our sight of him, the plainer it is that nevertheless he feels not so sure of the issue. He has a fight still to win. And the play is not over yet.

When he sees the figures of the women approaching the scene's tension rises instantly to high pitch. It is to be a long scene, of a struggle the deadlier for its quiet; even as wrestlers in a lock strain silently, motionless, until one is exhausted and as silently loosens grasp, and the match is over. The tension will hardly relax; a moment's relief, and it tightens again. The action is clearly articulated, deliberate, sparse; the speech indicates it and allows for it. Marcius is its firm and sensitive center. The argument ranges round him, widely, closely; touches him as husband, lover, father, son, Roman, uses his wife's tears, his boy's gallantly shrill defiance, Volumnia's desperate barring of the end to this road on which—it was she that set him. Silence is his ultimate answer; and the whole, with its passion, in its intimacies and simplicities, is keyed to the tenor of a great event.

Note the dramatic generalship with which Shakespeare employs his forces. First is the duel effect made by the mute, anonymous approach of the women, their speech, even for a moment their identity, held in reserve, while Marcius, describing them, at once interprets besides the effect made on him.[50] The battle begins and ends with a struggle within himself. It will end in silence; it

---

[50] The *in mourning habits* of the stage direction for this entrance is owed, apparently, to Capell. It implies veils, and is, I think, justified. The stage picture intended is not hard to reconstruct. Coriolanus will be seated at the council table on the inner stage surrounded by the contrastingly uniformed Volscian generals. The *Shout within* heralds the entry by a side door of the little group of veiled women and their attendants, who stand facing him and more or less with their backs to the audience, so that the "curtsy," and, upon Virgilia's unveiling, the "doves' eyes" and Volumnia's "bow" take effect more directly upon him than upon us. "Describing them"; I do not, of course, mean to imply to the Volscian generals, but to himself and to us, as the convention of that stage allowed.

begins articulately. Back and forth he is swayed; by the very sight, the first since his exile, of those three that he loves.[51]

> But out, affection!
> All bond and privilege of nature break!
> Let it be virtuous to be obstinate! . . .

Then, his wife's "doves' eyes" turned on him:

> I melt, and am not
> Of stronger earth than others. . . .

Lastly, to break the spell of Volumnia's grave obeisance, and against his boy's

> aspect of intercession, which
> Great nature cries, "Deny not." . . .

he violently flings away with

> Let the Volsces
> Plough Rome and harrow Italy; I'll never
> Be such a gosling to obey instinct, but stand
> As if a man were author of himself
> And knew no other kin.

But he is drawn to face Virgilia and her gentle

> My lord and husband.

to invite, with his repelling

> These eyes are not the same I wore in Rome.

her as gently keen

> The sorrow that delivers *us* thus changed
> Makes you think so.

He owns to the effect of the thrust:

> Like a dull actor now,
> I have forgot my part, and I am out,
> Even to a full disgrace. . . .

and, the next instant, she is in his arms.

---

[51] "Long as my exile. . . ," he says later. Actually how long Shakespeare leaves indeterminate; but while the suggestion, when he comes to Aufidius in Antium, is that he has lost little time in doing so, here and hereabouts the implication is that, at any rate, much has changed in his absence. There is no need at either juncture to be exact, so that—open inconsistency avoided—the dramatic best can be made of each calendar.

> Best of my flesh,
> Forgive my tyranny; but do not say
> For that "Forgive our Romans." O, a kiss,
> Long as my exile, sweet as my revenge!
> Now, by the jealous queen of heaven, that kiss
> I carried from thee, dear, and my true lip
> Hath virgined it e'er since. You gods! I prate. . . .

Much of Marcius is lit up in this. In his love for his wife a quality of nature rarer than that bred of the exchange of pride between him and his mother. From it had sprung at his triumphal entry into Rome the thought of the Volscian widows left desolate; the kindling touch of her lips might free him to sudden forgiveness now. Love and hate are near akin in him, are but the two sides of the one shield; and each he justifies by what he does, and that by what he is. To spend more words on either is to "prate."

He turns to

> the most noble mother of the world . . .

and with a

> Sink, my knee, i' the earth. . . .

gives her full due. She bids him

> stand up blest!

then kneels herself, thus "unproperly," she says, to

> Show duty, as mistaken all this while,
> Between the child and parent.

She shocks him, and means to. But the irony is rather in the event; and when he raises her she unconsciously gives it voice again:

> Thou art my warrior;
> I holp to frame thee.

She did indeed! As well her teaching as his learning has brought them to this pass.[52]

---

[52] This kneeling of each to other recalls Cordelia and King Lear. Shakespeare had found that in the old play about King Lear and his daughters. It clearly makes an affecting picture. Whether it was a favorite one with other dramatists of the time I am not well enough read to say. Whether or no, ceremonial kneeling was then in habitual use, and widely by comparison with the few occasions on which it is called for now.

Valeria, dignified, beautiful, silent—

> The noble sister of Publicola,
> The moon of Rome, chaste as the icicle
> That's curded by the frost from purest snow,
> And hangs on Dian's temple . . .

—follows in her place. Is she also to find her fate in the sack of a city?[53] Lastly the boy is put forward, sturdily stubborn, even against this great man his father's thrilling exhortation, until Volumnia takes order with a stern

> Your knee, sirrah!

and Marcius, delighting in him:

> That's my brave boy!

He, who has never counted the odds at which he fought, has never had to fight, surely, at such odds as this.

Volumnia, with due dignity, opens her plea. Upon its very threshold he stops her, the more petitionary himself in his denials:

> Do not bid me
> Dismiss my soldiers. . . .
>                    tell me not
> Wherein I seem unnatural, desire not
> To allay my rages and revenges. . . .

But she answers with an insistence matching his own:

> O, no more, no more!
> You have said you will not grant us any thing,
> For we have nothing else to ask but that
> Which you deny already. . . .

an obstinacy too:

> Yet we will ask. . . .

So he turns back to Aufidius and the Volsces, returns to their

---

[53] To suggest this, by her mere appearance in the scene, with, for aid, the gem-like phrase describing her put into Coriolanus' mouth, seems to be her only use to it. But it is an incidental use of some little value; and since Shakespeare had her available, why not bring her on? One may even speculate whether the part itself does not chiefly owe its existence to such a fact as that the King's Men had, at this juncture, a boy in the company, who could both look and act it well. Even in these, their well-furnished days, they were unlikely to be overburdened with that sort of thing.

council table, seats himself there again, as in judgment with
them.[54]

Her speech before this strange tribunal comes from a Volumnia
compelled at last to see Coriolanus' valor from the standpoint of
the vanquished. The exulting fierceness of her once-triumphant

> Death, that dark spirit, in 's nervy arm doth lie. . . .

has melted to the grief of

> Think with thyself
> How more unfortunate than all living women
> Are we come hither. . . .
> the mother, wife and child to see
> The son, the husband and the father tearing
> His country's bowels out. . . .

grief highly argued:

> thou barr'st us
> Our prayers to the gods. . . .
> for how can we,
> Alas! how can we for our country pray,
> Whereto we are bound, together with thy victory,
> Whereto we are bound? . . .

Yet out of the deadlock and division to which pride and wrath—
his fostering of it, and hers—have brought them, out of the fatal
dilemma—

> for either thou
> Must, as a foreign recreant, be led
> With manacles through our streets, or else
> Triumphantly tread on thy country's ruin. . . .

—she sees one way. But—Volumnia still!—her passion bids fair
to swamp her very plea for following it

> For myself, son . . .
> if I cannot persuade thee
> Rather to show a noble grace to both parts
> Than seek the end of one, thou shalt no sooner
> March to assault thy country than to tread—
> Trust to 't, thou shalt not—on thy mother's womb,
> That brought thee to this world.

[54] Note (once more) the visual effect of this, the contrast in the dress they
wear, he the single Roman among these Volsces.

Virgilia echoing her with

> Ay, and mine,
> That brought you forth this boy, to keep your name
> Living to time.

even the child, ridiculously, gallantly defiant:

> A' shall not tread on me;
> I'll run away till I am bigger, but then I'll fight.

Thus does this breed set about making peace.[55]

Marcius sits silent until the effect of the triply unanswerable challenge has died away. Then, quietly, reflectively, to the foiled self in him:

> Not of a woman's tenderness to be,
> Requires nor child nor woman's face to see.

And he rises and moves mechanically away, defeated and avoiding defeat. Volumnia's pursuing arguments sound strange to him; from her to him they well may! "Our suit is, that you reconcile . . ."! The Volsces are to say,

> "This mercy we have showed"; the Romans
> "This we received"; and each in either side
> Give the all-hail to thee, and cry "Be blest
> For making up this peace!"

*She* to be telling him:

> The end of war's uncertain. . . .

asking him:

> Thinkst thou it honourable for a noble man
> Still to remember wrongs?

Is this Volumnia?

---

[55] Were Shakespeare a didactic dramatist how well he might from this point build up his play to a moral and a happy ending: Marcius and his family reunited, Romans and Volsces clasping hands, peace over all! But he has the historic story to deal with (Plutarch is not to be lightly treated) and the tragedy it involves—which, however, we must remark, is a tragedy, not wholly of character, but of character and circumstance combined.

Volumnia (of all people) urges reconciliation. Coriolanus is not the man to sponsor that; he can at best, he feels, stand aside and "make convenient peace." But Aufidius also has to be reckoned with, and the Volscians who, for their part, want loot. It is in the fresh circumstances of the squabble over this that "character" once more plays Coriolanus false, and Aufidius can seize the chance to kill him.

It is here that his silence comes to be stressed by the baffled recurrence of her

> Speak to me, son. . . .
> Why dost not speak? . . .
> yet here he lets me prate
> Like one i' the stocks. . . .
> He turns away.

And the technique of the scene is in itself remarkable. Usually such a speech as this will concentrate our attention on the speaker; and, the more strongly, the less of even a side-glance from us can surrounding characters claim. But Volumnia makes Virgilia's tears, the child's high spirit, Valeria's quiet dignity a living part of the action, adding their eloquence in its kind to her own, to wield it all against the opposing silence of Marcius' last stand.

His silence counterbalances, and by a little will outbalance, her share in the encounter. For she ceases her attack, unbeaten but munition spent—

> I am husht until our city be a-fire,
> And then I'll speak a little.

—and still he has not answered.

> *Holds her by the hand, silent.*

is the stage direction, Shakespeare's own certainly. In the silence is his answer, and he spares her all other. She has won. And for him

> the heavens do ope,
> The gods look down, and this unnatural scene
> They laugh at. . . .

—unnatural, since pride and her pride in him have brought him to this, and she that helped make him is bidding him remake himself now. And that he can no longer do. Mercy and forgiveness are not for him. And it is she that has vanquished him. Only she could.

He gently warns her of what may follow:

> O, my mother, mother! O!
> You have won a happy victory to Rome;
> But for your son, believe it, O, believe it,

> Most dangerously you have with him prevailed
> If not most mortal to him. . . .

But, the great strain relaxed, she seemingly thinks but of her victory and does not heed. He braces himself again—as at the beginning of the struggle, so now to what must follow—with a

> But let it come.

next, pride abated, turns to Aufidius—out of all the world—for sympathy:

> Now, good Aufidius,
> Were you in my stead, would you have heard
> A mother less, or granted less, Aufidius?

—who, coldly observant, commits himself to no more than a

> I was moved withal.

and then comes to the decision that is to be his death:

> for my part,
> I'll not to Rome. I'll back with you; and pray you,
> Stand to me in this cause. . . .

Aufidius felt sure (we heard him say) that even those in Rome who feared Marcius most

> Will be as rash in the repeal, as hasty
> To expel him thence . . .

But if the traitor prefers conflict in Corioles, so much the worse for him—and the better for Aufidius!

It is not in Marcius to enter Rome again. For the last time—he knows to what he may be going—he lets himself be stirred to his depths:

> O, mother! wife!

After which, lest they should now catch up with his thoughts, should try, as it seems they will, to keep him there, he plays the man of affairs with them, the game loser:.

> Ay, by and by;
> But we will drink together, and you shall bear
> A better witness back than words. . . .

Gallantly courteous, he addresses the whole train:

> Ladies, you deserve
> To have a temple built to you: all the swords
> In Italy, and her confederate arms,
> Could not have made this peace.

## ROME DELIVERED

Rome fearfully awaits news of her fate. *We* already know it, so the suspense must not be spun out. Menenius returning meets Sicinius, while the issue is still, he supposes, in doubt, and he can avenge on him his own repulse by assurance that Volumnia will do no better. The old Tribune is in despair:

> He loved his mother dearly.

and Menenius finds satisfaction of the perverser sort in:

> So did he me; and he no more remembers his mother now than an eight-year-old horse. The tartness of his face sours ripe grapes. . . . Mark what mercy his mother shall bring from him: there is no more mercy in him than there is milk in a male tiger; that shall our poor city find. . . .

and so falls back upon

> all this is long of you.

There comes yet more for him in a messenger's tidings that the Plebeians have now seized upon the wretched Brutus,

> And hale him up and down; all swearing, if
> The Roman ladies bring not comfort home,
> They'll give him death by inches.

So when the good news arrives that

> the ladies have prevailed,
> The Volscians are dislodged, and Marcius gone. . . .

he can but be at first a trifle disappointed. Sicinius, for his part, who would not credit the bad news when it came, is wary of the good news now.

> Friend,
> Art thou certain this is true? is it most certain?

But the rejoicing sounds without are evidence enough:

> *Trumpets, hoboyes, drums beate altogether.*

Shakespeare's theater can do no more. From Menenius, then, breaks a generously happy

> This is good news:
> I will go meet the ladies. This Volumnia
> Is worth of consuls, senators, patricians,
> A city full . . .

with, for a last humorous gibe,

> of Tribunes, such as you,
> A sea and land full.

and he is away.[56]

Sicinius, so barely saved, must reassert his dignity:

> First, the gods bless you for your tidings; next,
> Accept *my* thankfulness.

The Messenger, afflicted by no such pomposity:

> Sir, we have all
> Great cause to give great thanks.

Rome's saviors near the city; at point to enter! A Tribune's benign presence is called for:

> We will meet them,
> And help the joy.

## VOLUMNIA'S TRIUMPH

*Enter two Senators, with Ladies, passing over the stage, with other Lords.*

Thus this short stretch of the action ends, with such a procession, so acclaimed, as that which once brought Coriolanus back in triumph from his wars. And the people are to

> Unshout the noise that banished Marcius,
> Repeal him with the welcome of his mother. . . .

—but too late.

## THE END

*Enter Tullus Aufidius with Attendants.*

—the *Attendants* an opening suggestion of authority.

---

[56] The Folio's stage directions leave him, by default, included in the general *Exeunt* a few lines later. But clearly he does not wait for Sicinius.

Aufidius gives the tone to this, the play's last scene. Its doings are to win him success, and he promptly assumes control of them:

> Go tell the lords o' the city I am here;
> Deliver them this paper: having read it,
> Bid them repair to the market place. . . .
>                     Him I accuse
> The city ports by this hath entered, and
> Intends to appear before the people, hoping
> To purge himself with words. Dispatch.

Of all men, Coriolanus, "to appear before the people" that he may "purge himself with words"! The attendants go about the business given them, and are replaced by

> *3 or 4 Conspirators of Aufidius' Faction.*

and he and they proceed to make the case against Coriolanus.

Aufidius is an injured man, and although

> We must proceed as we do find the people.

—as troublesome in Corioles as in Rome apparently—it should not be hard to show him a wronged man. Such generosity as he has shown, with such advantage taken of it! For the "witchcraft," we may note, which once made men "fly to the Roman"—Aufidius among them!—has now become the

>                     dews of flattery,
> Seducing so my friends . . .

And, above all,

> When he had carried Rome, and that we looked
> For no less spoil than glory—

for this, at least, Aufidius promises,

>         my sinews shall be stretched upon him. . . .
>         he sold the blood and labour
> Of our great action; therefore he shall die,
> And I'll renew me in his fall. . . .

—at which moment

> *Drums and trumpets sound, with great shouts of the people.*

So Marcius comes in triumph, if not back to Rome, into Corioles. His rival stands to listen. And, were more provocation needed, friends provide it in their low reminder that

> Your native town you entered like a post,
> And had no welcomes home; but he returns
> Splitting the air with noise.
>                          And patient fools,
> Whose children he hath slain, their base throats tear
> With giving him glory.

The lords of the city, now arriving, offer their welcome, none
the less—which Aufidius, with a certain sulky modesty, disclaims.
More to the purpose, they have digested his charges against
Marcius, the last that he should

> give away
> The benefit of our levies, answering us
> With our own charge: making a treaty where
> There was a yielding; this admits no excuse.

and Aufidius can afford to stand aside; with an

> He approaches: you shall hear him.

Note now the stage direction:

> *Enter Coriolanus marching with drum and colours; the
> Commoners being with him.*

He is in full panoply of war, an impressive, a commanding figure.
This is he to whose side Aufidius' soldiers flocked. Aufidius himself looks and will feel nothing beside him. Moreover, the
commoners are with him, to cheer or hoot him, as the Roman
commoners did. They are cheering him now. And whatever the
Volscian case against him, he means to make a good one for
himself. But it is a hardened Marcius that makes it:

> Hail, lords! I am returned your soldier,
> No more infected with my country's love
> Than when I parted hence, but still subsisting
> Under your great command. . . .

a Marcius brought to claiming that

> Our spoils we have brought home
> Doth more than counterpoise a full third part
> The charges of the action. . . .

—the man of whom it could be said in Rome that

> Our spoils he kicked at,
> And looked upon things precious as they were
> The common muck of the world. . . .

Not that a third of the cost of the war is matter of great account either! But he means to make himself a place here too. He must. He has no other left.

Aufidius sees this, and that he must strike hard, and without delay. "Traitor" is a sharp blow; and the derisive "Marcius" added—

> Ay, Marcius, Caius Marcius. Dost thou think
> I'll grace thee with that robbery, thy stolen name
> Coriolanus in Corioles?

—will draw his enemy towards tricky ground. He says no word of his own wrongs; only that:

> You lords and heads o' the state, perfidiously
> He has betrayed your business, and given up,
> For certain drops of salt, your city Rome,
> I say "your city". . . .

The commoners are listening too, the conspirators are on the watch. Aufidius drives on:

> Breaking his oath and resolution like
> A twist of rotten silk . .
> He whined and roared away your victory. . . .

To all of which Coriolanus has reasonable answer. But the insults to his soldiership, his manhood, blot out all else:

> Hear'st thou, Mars?

Aufidius ends with a contemptuous

> Name not the god, thou boy of tears. . . .
> No more.

Marcius, incandescent with anger:

> Measureless liar, thou hast made my heart
> Too great for what contains it. . . .

yet it is the "boy" that has pricked deepest, and the more intolerably for the truth of it. Of the lies let these "grave lords" judge; but for the liar himself:

> Who wears my stripes impressed upon him, that
> Must bear my beating to his grave . . .

Here is the old exultant—that boyishly exultant—Marcius. Let his enemies take vengeance on him if they will:

> Cut me to pieces, Volsces; men and lads,
> Stain all your edges on me. . . .

for

> If you have writ your annals true, 'tis there,
> That, like an eagle in a dove-cote, I
> Fluttered your Volscians in Corioles:
> Alone I did it. Boy!

One of Shakespeare's master-moments this, in which he brings the tragic figure to the very edge of the ridiculous, but stays him there.

Even as his friends in Rome were wont to check and save him, so might the Volscian lords, would he but let them:

> The man is noble, and his fame folds in
> This orb o' the earth. His last offence to us
> Shall have judicious hearing. . . .

But Aufidius, who while he rages can still calculate, in appealing to them is appealing over their heads to the commoners, those commoners that, in Corioles as in Rome, Coriolanus will so obligingly provoke for him:

> Why, noble lords,
> Will you be put in mind of his blind fortune,
> Which was your shame, by this unholy braggart,
> 'Fore your own eyes and ears?

It is the conspirators' cue for a fomenting

> Let him die for 't.

and, as once before, the mob howls for his blood. As once before too he draws his sword, disdaining aid:

> O! that I had him,
> With six Aufidiuses, or more, his tribe,
> To use my lawful sword.

An "Insolent villain!" from Aufidius gives the conspirators their cue again; and, with vociferous "Kills" to drown the cries of "Hold!", they crowd in on him, daggers drawn. He falls, and

*Aufidius stands on him.*

He stands on him! Could words say more?
　His first thought is to justify his deed—

> My noble masters, hear me speak.

—and not until he hears the shocked reproaches does he realize
what he is shamefully doing now.

> O, Tullus! . . .
> Tread not upon him. Masters, all be quiet.
> Put up your swords.

But it will not be so difficult to persuade moderate men that,
though it has been wrong to kill him, yet Coriolanus is better
dead. Therefore

> Bear from hence his body,
> And mourn you for him. Let him be regarded
> As the most noble corse that ever herald
> Did follow to his urn.

The Second Lord already sees clearly the other side of the matter:

> His own impatience
> Takes from Aufidius a great part of blame.
> Let's make the best of it.

and Aufidius adds in all sincerity:

> My rage is gone,
> And I am struck with sorrow.

# The Verse

IN listening to the play we shall be conscious of the verse as a
thing in itself only at certain intenser moments, which are thus—
by one metrical device or another—emphasized and made
memorable. For the rest it will impress us rather as powerful,
rounded speech, resonant somewhat above the ordinary, and, in
particular, borne forward by a most compelling rhythm. A
change from verse to prose, even, we may chiefly remark as a
change of temper, a lessening of emotional pressure, or merely
a timely contrast.

Not for long now—by the measure of his swift development—
has Shakespeare habitually dealt in "set pieces" of verse, "Queen
Mab" speeches, pronouncements that "All the world's a stage" or

that "The quality of mercy is not strained"; and, even when he did, they would seldom lack some direct dramatic sanction. Portia's, for instance, is legitimate forensic eloquence, and Jaques has been cast, in the Arden pastoral, for the part of moralizer-in-chief to the banished Duke. Again, the speeches of the two Henrys upon sleeplessness, ceremony and kingship may, in method, be more rhetorical than reflective, but they suit both character and occasion. A little later, Brutus' ordered soliloquies come as the due expression of an ordered mind, and Mark Antony's oratory is directed first to his Roman hearers, and only through them upon us, the audience; and let actor or audience forget this and its dramatic purpose is warped. Then, with *Hamlet*—and in Hamlet's own speech particularly—we come within reach of a seeming spontaneity. Shakespeare allows him all possible scope of expression, both in prose and verse; and in the choice between them, and in the form and color of the verse as well as in its content, his every mood, of contemplation, irony or despair, will be sensitively reflected. It is, of course, only a "seeming spontaneity." People do not naturally speak verse, be it but blank verse; and even in prose, and for the simple speech of citizen or peasant, Shakespeare never lapses into an *imitated* spontaneity, so to forfeit all the aids of form and accepted convention.[57]

It is a consonant part—this reaching towards a seeming spontaneity—of Shakespeare's general development as a dramatist, and it necessarily tends to loosen and even break down the form of the verse. To begin with he is a poet writing plays—as Marlowe was, and Lyly—and his lengths of verse, often narrative or descriptive in their bent, will readily fall into regular form. And for long enough the form, a little eased or a little fortified, accommodates the direct expression of character and emotion very well, as, for instance, in the forthright Hotspur, less well for the subtler Richard II. It is when character and emotion gain complexity and extraordinary force that—as a stream in flood eats

[57] An earlier instance of this "seeming spontaneity" in verse can be found in the Nurse in *Romeo and Juliet*. Really, it sometimes seems as if Shakespeare must have had all the secrets of his art stored in him from the beginning, as if he had only to enlarge upon what he already knew.

its banks away—the verse breaks bounds; then Shakespeare himself has developed from the poet writing plays into the true dramatic poet.

This is not a quibbling distinction, it indicates a very fertile difference. Incidentally, it overrides the question of the medium used, prose or verse. *Macbeth* could have been written in prose without fundamental loss; it is poetically conceived. There is as much poetry in the prose of *As You Like It* as in its verse.[58] Convention and convenience, both to the dramatist and his actors, will commonly have recommended verse; but from the beginning Shakespeare seemingly tended to use whichever, that or prose, better suited his immediate purpose.[59] Shylock's supreme outburst is in prose; there is dramatic value in the mere contrast with the mellifluous verse surrounding it. *Richard II*'s exceptional uniformity of verse remains unbroken, though we might look for prose in the short gardeners' scene. Bottom and Weaver and his friends demand prose, if only because they have a play to rehearse and perform. Its medium must not be their own, and it will go best in doggerel. But who that could write verse would not write it for the rest of *A Midsummer Night's Dream*? Prose suits Falstaff to perfection; and Beatrice and Benedick, Rosalind and Orlando, leave the verse of the plays they animate sounding dull by comparison. But, comedy yielding to tragedy, verse comes to its own again; since it can excite emotion and sustain illusion as prose cannot.

The verse must not, in its new-won freedom, be let flow too freely, too slackly, or it will lose its power—as did so much of the verse of Shakespeare's immediate successors; and when Dryden and his school thought at last to come to the rescue the mischief had gone too far. With Shakespeare himself there will always be some recurrent check, in the shape of a line or a passage of stricter meter. Not mechanically inserted; if dramatic demand breaks the form of the verse, dramatic demand will also restore it. Hamlet is recalled from the overflowing emotion of

---

[58] Without *fundamental* loss: for some proof of this see Maeterlinck's translation of *Macbeth*. And Dover Wilson discovers in *As You Like It* the fossils of a verse version, of which Shakespeare presumably thought better.

[59] "Convention and convenience": Blank verse may well, with a little practice, prove easier to write than formal prose; it is certainly easier to learn.

> Bloody, bawdy villain!
> Remorseless, treacherous, lecherous, kindless villain!
> O, vengeance!

to the controlled thought of

> About my brain! I have heard
> That guilty creatures, sitting at a play,
> Have by the very cunning of the scene . . .

And the firm rhythm of Othello's

> Farewell the tranquil mind! farewell content!
> Farewell the plumed troop and the big wars. . . .

or of his

> It is the cause, it is the cause, my soul:
> Let me not name it to you, you chaste stars! . . .

—with other such counterbalancings to the succession of minor
metrical liberties lodged (inconspicuously for the most part) in
the general run of the verse—help to keep him heroically
dominant over the commoner traffic of the play. The larger the
liberties taken, the greater the need for this recurrent control.
For drama is a disciplined art, hedged in by a hundred restrictions.
It is akin to poetry and to verse in that, and the restrictions themselves are akin. And in the poetic play a loosening of the ties of
verse only leaves it to depend the more upon a more essential
order of character and idea, upon which—and not chiefly upon
form—it must in fact be built. But this will be essentially poetic
and dramatic too since it will deal with the metaphysical things
with which poetry most properly deals, and with conflicts of the
human will. Shakespeare evolves, then, for the major medium of
his maturer plays, this enfranchised verse; a rhythmic and
melodious speech, powerful and malleable at once. Of its form
we shall often be but indefinitely aware; as much is kept as will
keep the structure intact, now more, now less being needed.
Little sense of artifice is left to intervene between us and the acted
play; the medium grows transparent. Sacrificing none of them, he
molds his diversity of means into a unity of dramatic expression;
and he lifts us—we have only to surrender—to the level of it.

Not much is to be gained—in appreciation, that is to say, of its
living qualities—by carrying such verse, cold and dead, to the

dissecting table, there to demonstrate its spondees and dactyls, its overrun lines and feminine endings. Assuredly Shakespeare never planned it so; and, multiply rules as we may in trying to round his practice into some sort of system, the exceptions will outrun them. We do not think in terms of prosody at all of

> I am dying, Egypt, dying; only
> I here importune death awhile, until
> Of many thousand kisses the poor last
> I lay upon thy lips.

noting, as we speak the lines, that the first has—rather surprisingly —the orthodox ten syllables; nor do we remember Lear's

> Never, never, never, never, never!

as five successive trochees. Form and meaning are not to be separated.

But for all the freedom in the general run of the verse the later plays furnish us still with rhymed couplets enough, "sentences," lengths of octosyllabics, and such like conventional forms. There is the difference, however, that these things now owe their place to some particular dramatic use that can be made of them—to clinch an argument, stress a desperate moment or clarify a reflective one.[60] And the use is overt; the effect made will stand out like a patch of bright color, or, if the main speech-fabric hereabouts is already brightly colored, of contrasting shade. Shakespeare never abandons a well-tried dramatic device; let it still serve his purpose, that is the only test.

One freedom opens up another. Individual expression besides, the verse may now be molded to the character of particular scenes, or of the play itself. The fantastic rhyming of Edgar and the Fool, attuned to Lear's own lunacy, does much for the storm-scenes in *King Lear*. The verse of *Othello* combines energy and color and ease in a manner of its own. And contrast in color and in rhythm generally is to be added to the others between *Antony and Cleopatra* and *Coriolanus*. Imperial Rome and exotic Egypt

---

[60] And here, it may be added, at the very opening of *Coriolanus*, is a "set piece," in the story of the Belly and the Members. But it is put to direct dramatic use. The picture of Menenius cajoling the assembled citizens, to be contrasted immediately after with Marcius' swift hard way with them—the two passages together serve as a sort of opening statement of this aspect of the play.

and the searching minds and sweeping passions which inform them—the magnificent many-faceted verse of the one reflects these, even as concentration on a narrower strife finds fitting voice in the closer woven, more angular, lines of *Coriolanus*.

There is little in subject or characters to carry Shakespeare off his feet and set the verse of *Coriolanus* soaring. Egoism, rivalry, cunning and pride (the more generous traits, making by comparison a poor show) leave the radiant passages few, incidental usually and as likely as not to illuminate some minor figure.

> Now the fair goddess Fortune
> Fall deep in love with thee: and her great charms
> Misguide thy opposers' swords! Bold gentleman,
> Prosperity be thy page!

—the old warrior, himself outdone, but lavish in admiration of his heroically truculent young comrade; those few lines brighten the whole scene. And it is to an anonymous messenger that is given the brilliant little

> 'Tis thought
> That Marcius shall be Consul.
> I've seen the dumb men throng to see him, and
> The blind to hear him speak: matrons flung gloves,
> Ladies and maids their scarfs and handkerchers,
> Upon him as he passed: the nobles bended
> As to Jove's statue, and the commons made
> A shower and thunder with their caps and shouts:
> I never saw the like.[61]

## DRAMATIC VERSE INDEED

The verse in the main is vigorous, and it drives hard and exclusively at its dramatic purpose. The rhythm is apt to be of more import than the melody. The words are often unmusical in themselves, and they may be crushed into the lines like fuel to stoke a furnace. It is a cast of speech well fitting the reason-searching strife which pervades the play; and none in the canon

---

[61] It is evident, I think, that for the later plays Shakespeare had actors who could be relied upon to make good effect with these small but striking parts. There are several others in *Coriolanus*, some in *King Lear*, and a dozen or more in *Antony and Cleopatra*. They were doubled no doubt.

is fuller of quarrel of one sort or another from beginning to end.

But if the verse—with nothing in the matter of it to stir the imagination—does not soar, neither does it ever sag. The play in this respect has not a single weak spot. One detects, in the frequent lack of clarity, a certain effort in the writing; but at least the effort is never shirked. The most patent instance comes, perhaps, in Aufidius' summary of his rival's failings:

> Whether 'twas pride,
> Which out of daily fortune ever taints
> The happy man; whether defect of judgment,
> To fail in the disposing of those chances
> Which he was lord of; or whether nature,
> Not to be other than one thing, not moving
> From th' casque to th' cushion, but commanding peace
> Even with the same austerity and garb
> As he controlled the war; but one of these,
> As he hath spices of them all—not all,
> For I dare so far free him—made him feared,
> So hated and so banished. . . .

—and so on, until the long succession of saving clauses is tied off in a complex aphorism.[62] If Shakespeare could not render down his thought into something clearer than this he might better, surely, have omitted the passage altogether. But no; Aufidius at this point, he feels, needs rationalizing, Coriolanus too. And if the idea involved will not distill and flow freely, it must just be wrung out. It cannot be omitted, and a flaw left in the fabric of thought.

Clarity yields to intensity. Witness Sicinius' malignly prescient

> Doubt not
> The commoners for whom we stand, but they
> Upon their ancient malice will forget
> With the least cause these his new honours; which
> That he will give them, make I as little question
> As he is proud to do't.

Put on paper, the last part of this may not parse well. But in speech, if the speaker be skillful, the thoughts themselves can be

---

[62] There is corruption in the text of the closing lines. But its elucidating would still leave the passage as a whole far from clear.

related—the "which" linked to the "least cause," the "proud" given its proper prominence—and the very lack of clarity be made to suggest their urgency.

Volumnia's disingenuous arguments, which send Marcius back to the market place, are wound out smoothly:

> If it be honour in your wars to seem
> The same you are not . . .
>               now it lies on you to speak
> To the people; not by your own instruction,
> Nor by the matter which your heart prompts you,
> But with such words that are but roted in
> Your tongue, though but bastards and syllables
> Of no allowance to your bosom's truth.
> Now this no more dishonours you at all . . .

—the verse cold, sustained, regular, unmelodious, fitted to the occasion and her temper, its sense aridly clear.

The man himself, if but a worse side of him, is alive both in the matter and manner of Marcius' beginning:

> What's the matter, you dissentious rogues,
> That, rubbing the poor itch of your opinion,
> Make yourselves scabs?

with its curt "What's the matter?", its veritably physical repugnance for the "rogues" set in the ugly images which follow, these followed the next moment by

> What would you have, you curs,
> That like not peace nor war? The one affrights you,
> The other makes you proud. He that trusts to you,
> When he should find you lions, finds you hares;
> Where foxes, geese: you are no surer, no,
> Than is the coal of fire upon the ice,
> Or hailstone in the sun.

with its banging-about of contraries, like so many boxes on the ear; the scolding then carried on into the crowded, contemptuous

> Hang 'em! They say!
> They'll sit by the fire, and presume to know
> What's done i' the Capitol; who's like to rise,
> Who thrives, and who declines; side factions, and give out
> Conjectural marriages. . . .

together with such tunelessness as is in "hunger broke stone walls," "horns o' the moon," "insurrection's arguing"—suitably, not a line of clear melody or smooth rhythm.

Further than which—one may at this point note—in the shaping and attuning of his verse to the expression of *individual* character, Shakespeare, here or elsewhere, in this play or another, hardly goes. For there must be some prevailing unity of form, or a play would fall in pieces; so, whatever the liberty given to the verse, its ten-syllable, five-stress foundation is left (as we have seen already) solidly underlying it still. And characters, even at their most individual, are still only emergent from type; this is true of Hamlet, of Falstaff even, Rosalind or Beatrice. Coriolanus himself is a variation of the soldier-hero, Aufidius of a villainous rival, while Menenius fills—if overfills—the place of the worldly-wise old counsellor, and Volumnia traces a little less theatrical descent as Roman matron. And the scope and individual character of all dramatic speech, be this remembered, since it must be instantly understood, has its limits there.

Dialogue and action are made to interpret one the other with exact economy. We actually see, first the failure, then the exciting success of the attack on Corioles, the city's capture and its token sacking; and with this goes no more dialogue than is needed—a bare line or two might at a pinch be omitted—for illustration. Cominius in six lines—

> Breathe you, my friends: well fought; we are come off
> Like Romans, neither foolish in our stands,
> Nor cowardly in retire: believe me, sirs,
> We shall be charged again. Whiles we have struck,
> By interims and conveying gusts we have heard
> The charges of our friends.

—is made to tell us what we need to know of his share in the battle and its further prospects, to paint us himself as general (just such a one as Marcius is not; the contrast striking), to tell us something besides of the lie of the battlefield, even of the weather! When Corioles has been taken, and Marcius is speeding Cominius' aid and the discomfiture of Aufidius, old Titus Lartius, with him his general's drummer and trumpeter, a scout also,

distinguished by his light running gear, come from the inner to
the outer stage, an officer and some more soldiers following:

> So, let the ports be guarded: keep your duties
> As I have set them down. If I do send, dispatch
> Those centuries to our aid; the rest will serve
> For a short holding; if we lose the field,
> We cannot keep the town. . . .
> Hence, and shut your gates upon us.
> Our guider, come; to the Roman camp conduct us.

Seven lines of speech, together with the significance of the figures
and their movement—away from the city: back into it; the closing
of the gates—suffice for this taste of Roman caution and cool
judgment in warfare. The contrast is to come this time in the next
scene's furious duel between Marcius and Aufidius.

The verse in general is meaty and lean; it contains few images
and is all but free of extended metaphor. Its quality of direct
attack is a strength to the actor. As an instance:

> Officious, and not valiant; you have shamed me
> In your condemned seconds.

—for Aufidius, left standing there while Marcius triumphantly
pursues the unwelcome interlopers, the least wordiness would
seem weakness; but that one spare sentence an actor can pack with
spleen.

Marcius' magnanimity is given as direct and simple expression.
The battle over:

> I sometime lay here in Corioles
> At a poor man's house; he used me kindly.
> He cried to me; I saw him prisoner.
> But then Aufidius was within my view,
> And wrath o'erwhelmed my pity. I request you
> To give my poor host freedom.

It makes part—with the immediate weary-minded forgetting of
the man's name; has he not the right to be weary!—of the up-
building of his character, is a counterpart to that scornful rating
of the commoners. And the verse accommodates this; as it does
his joking response to the army's acclaim of him:

> I will go wash;
> And when my face is fair you shall perceive
> Whether I blush or no.

as it will later his lovingly ironic reproof to his wife's tears of welcome:

> Wouldst thou have laughed had I come coffin'd home,
> That weeps't to see me triumph? ...

Surely the very perfection of such simplicity!

The play contains little or no superfluous matter. With the civic struggle at full pitch, the effect to be made one of riot and confusion, each character, either chorus of Senators and plebeians, contributes exactly to the scene's need.

BRUTUS.                   Aediles, seize him!

CITIZENS.    Yield, Marcius, yield!

MENENIUS.                 Hear me one word;
             Beseech you, Tribunes, hear me but one word.

AEDILES.     Peace, peace!

MENENIUS.    Be that you seem, truly your country's friend,
             And temperately proceed to what you would
             Thus violently redress.

BRUTUS.                 Sir, these cold ways,
             That seem like prudent helps, are very poisonous
             Where the disease is violent. Lay hands upon
               him,
             And bear him to the rock.

MARCIUS.                 No, I'll die here.
             There's some among you have beheld me
               fighting:
             Come, try upon yourselves what you have seen
               me.

MENENIUS.    Down with that sword! Tribunes, withdraw
               awhile.

BRUTUS.    Lay hands upon him.

MENENIUS.                 Help Marcius! Help!
             You that be noble, help him, young and old!

CITIZENS.    Down with him! Down with him!

*In this mutiny, the Tribunes, the Aediles, and the People
are beat in.*

The passage is scored as it might be for an orchestra, each instrument given its task: Brutus' sharp order, reinforced by the plebeians' shout; Menenius' half-heard remonstrance; the Aediles' command for the silence in which Menenius and Brutus exchange their acid arguments; this sharply broken again by Brutus. And no shout follows now; since Marcius, mute and motionless so far, suddenly draws his sword and challenges combat. Circumspect old Menenius presses peace on both parties. It is Brutus who is reckless and hounds on his outnumbering mob. Then, for Menenius, if it is to come to fighting, each must stand to his own side. And the fit few prove too much for the many.

## THE DYNAMIC PHRASE

Spare dialogue need not be poor dialogue. The little said can be made to suggest much left unsaid. Dramatic art matures to this. In the cruder sort of play the characters will often not be fully dramatized, the dramatist himself to be heard speaking through them too plainly. But when they are, and their speech is authentically their own, then, by planning and a close collaboration with the actor, it can be brought to the expression of the implicit too, of those confusions of thought that trouble men, of feelings that never, in life, find words. The expression must be kept seemingly lifelike, not translated into overexplicit—into explanatory—terms: this would falsify the effect of it. The art of the dramatist lies in the discovering of more covert means.

The dynamic phrase, into which the actor is to pack the effect of a cumulated mass of thought and feeling, is one means. Shakespeare early learned the use of it. When Romeo hears of Juliet's death:

Is it even so? Then I defy you, stars!

rhetoric will follow later; but nothing of such deep and suggestive feeling. Falstaff's

Master Shallow, I owe you a thousand pound.

is a line of the sort, with its comically generous divining of Master Shallow's feelings too. So, when he has watched Cressid dallying with Diomed, is Troilus' response to Ulysses' "All's done, my lord," his grim "It is."

The dynamic phrase can be used in more ways than one. And there is purer tragedy in Macduff's cold

He has no children.

than in all his throbbing grief for his loss of them. Macbeth's own response to what once his servants would hardly have dared tell him:

> The Queen, my lord, is dead.

is no more than a silence, to be followed—when that bitter emptiness, his loss of the very power to feel, has made itself felt—by the wearily impatient

> She should have died hereafter:
> There would have been a time for such a word. . . .

and some detached reflections upon the meaninglessness of life. The effect—as of spiritual impotence—is not simply in these. To gain it, the underlying tragedy has been the play's length in development.

In a play, text apart from context may lose most of its meaning. The story itself, with Shakespeare, will run directly and openly along; there is no plot (the term will be misleading) to be spun and unraveled.[63] The play's structure is built up by the inter-locking of character and event, and the opposition of character to character; this gives it body, balance and strength. In *Coriolanus* the main stresses are between Marcius and the Senate on the one side, the people on the other; this beside, between Marcius and Aufidius, Marcius and Volumnia, jolly Menenius and the sour Tribunes. These are plain to be seen, and they implement the action. But there is much of auxiliary consequence as well, not set out at length or very explicitly, left latent, rather, for the actors to develop or elucidate in their acting.

The dramatist plans the essentials of this auxiliary action. Directions for it will be implicit in those passages of thrifty dialogue and their context; but only as realized and expanded will its full significance be made clear. When, for instance, in the play's first scene Marcius and Cominius and the Senators come together, their conduct to each other, the friendly yielding of precedence, Marcius' show of respect for the Consul and "our best elders," his easy acceptance otherwise of his own heroic eminence, and (pointed omission telling too) the ignoring of the

---

63 *Othello*, among the greater plays, really the single exception, nor fully an exception even so.

new Tribunes—twenty pregnant lines and their acting suffice to picture us men and party; and not even the anonymous among them are left lay figures.

So it is with the triumphal entry after the victory at Corioles. Action and speech are knit together, the one clarifying and enhancing the other. The shouts of welcome hushed, Marcius' look is turned—ours too again—to the women modestly withdrawn there; Roman mother and wife, the harsh Volumnia shaken by emotion, Virgilia happily weeping. Then he, Rome's hero, kneels dutifully to his mother, dries his wife's tears with words of gentle, magnanimously grave irony, frees himself from that mood with a joke for Menenius, his courteous bow to Valeria. More telling too will be this second ignoring of the Tribunes (on a third occasion, Marcius, confident of his consulship, will openly voice his contempt for them). Again, it is a matter of thirty-five lines or less. Yet not only their own significance, their illustration and the interplay of the response they demand, brings every participant in the scene into helping to give it life.

Shakespeare has come to demanding more of his actors, and to giving them more—though it may be less ostensible—opportunity. He demands their imaginative collaboration, leaves much to their discretion, gives them outlines to color in lightly or heavily. How large a part, for instance, does wine-flushed stubbornness play in Aufidius' repeated refusal to recognize the unmuffled Marcius, waiting by his hearth in Antium? The actor may decide. The text leaves him latitude and discretion, Shakespeare providing neither comment nor response to clinch the matter.

When Menenius returns with Volumnia and Virgilia from parting with the banished Marcius at the city gate: the strain now relaxed, the day lost, old age in him suddenly gives way; and against their vituperatings he can only set a "Peace, peace! be not so loud," a "Come, come; peace!"; and finally, the triumphant Tribunes departing, a

> You have told them home;
> And, by my troth, you have cause. You'll sup with me?

With no more to be done, there's left at least the comfort of a meal! The mere words given their surface meaning do little more than somewhat superfluously help the action on. But as bits of material to be used for filling out the figure of Menenius a skillful actor can put them to lively use. And that final consolatory bidding to supper then becomes also the better springboard for the grim, indomitable

> Anger's my meat; I sup upon myself,
> And so shall starve with feeding.

by which—its immediate effect besides—we shall be helped to keep Volumnia vividly in mind during her coming absence from the action.

The actor thus potently collaborating, one scene can be made to feed others that follow, and repeated expounding be avoided. Aufidius' backsliding from Marcius as they march together upon Rome is fully set out in his talk with his Lieutenant. After this merely his watchful presence through successive scenes will be eloquent, and the few cold phrases with which he breaks its silence need no enlarging: for example, his dry approbation of Marcius' rebuffing of Menenius with that

> You keep a constant temper.

his ironic sympathy for the son's breaking at last under the mother's pleading:

> I was moved withal.

A moment later comes an aside as explicit as was the talk with the Lieutenant:

> I am glad thou hast set thy mercy and thy honour
> At difference in thee: out of that I'll work
> Myself a former fortune.

and this keeps the trend of the action incontestably clear. But his open share in the two scenes, those two dry sentences (and one other) which positively do little more than emphasize his continuing presence, these an Aufidius can discreetly color, can most effectively charge with the strange blend of hatred and admiration that we know possesses the man. Such acting it is that adds something of another dimension to the personified narrative of a play, a dimension of being.

A speech may have an auxiliary sense, to which the actor must give value by his own particular means. When Marcius has finally yielded Rome's fate to Volumnia's plea he knows—and we are aware—that he has also put his own in Aufidius' hands. He turns to him:

> Aufidius, though I cannot make true wars,
> I'll frame convenient peace. Now, good Aufidius,
> Were you in my stead, would you have heard
> A mother less, or granted less, Aufidius?

The expressed resolve beside, in the mere repetitions of that "Aufidius," as the actor can give them varying cadence, will sound all the pleading on his own behalf—it is little!—that Marcius' pride could ever let him make.

To hark back to his banishment: much of the preceding scene is but preparation for the promised self-control of the curt

> I am content.

with which on his return to the market place he answers the Tribunes' provocative demand:

> If you submit you to the people's voices,
> Allow their officers, and are content
> To suffer lawful censure for such faults
> As shall be proved upon you?

for the countering too, a little later, of a yet more insolently peremptory

> Answer to us.

with the measured

> Say then; 'tis true. I ought so.

Such effects of self-control can, it is obvious, only be convincingly made when the elements of something to control have already been as convincingly built into the character.

## THE USE OF SILENCE

Shakespeare has learned to put silence to a variety of uses. Although, later in this same scene, intolerably stung by that "traitor to the people," Marcius finally forswears his promised temperance, yet he stands rigidly silent while Sicinius

> in the name o' the people,
> And in the power of us the Tribunes . . .

passes formal sentence of banishment upon him, while the people ratify it with a chorused

> It shall be so.

Thus he multiplies many times—when anger finally does break bounds—the effect of his

> You common cry of curs! whose breath I hate . . .

And there is the silence to which the unhappy Tribunes are reduced when, while Cominius and Menenius mock them, the news accumulates that this once banished Marcius is marching with the Volscians upon Rome—one meek

> But is this true, sir?

from Brutus, put in to emphasize it. There is most particularly the

> *Holds her by the hand, silent.*

—Shakespeare's own direction, that rarity! It is no more than a simple gesture, with which Marcius accepts the doom his surrender to his mother brings on him; a mere silence, yet it is the culminating moment of the play.

In the vivifying of such silences, the imaginative use of the "dynamic phrase" with its pent emotions, expressing things left latent, in the general demand now made upon the actor that he altogether assimilate himself to the character he is presenting, much is changed from the earlier illustrative declaiming of verse or prose. Yet Shakespeare's is, and remains through all changes, the drama of eloquence. And his art's chief achievement in this kind has been to turn eloquence for its own sake into a *relative* eloquence (so to call it) springing, seemingly spontaneously, from character-enlivening occasion; the poetic form not broken, set free rather to be as personal and malleable a medium of expression as may be.

## DRAMATICALLY LEGITIMATE ELOQUENCE

The story of *Coriolanus* is pre-eminently one of public life; and throughout the play—from Menenius' persuasive tale of the Belly and the Members to Marcius' last desperate haranguing of his Volscian masters—scene after scene offers dramatically legitimate occasion for eloquence. There is much variety of occasion too, as of speaker and temper of speech; the mutiny of the citizens, so differently dealt with by Menenius and Marcius; the crisis on the battlefield, the thanks to Marcius for his great part in the victory, later the public address to him with its carefully sought phrases; the war of words between Marcius and the Tribunes; Volumnia's spitfire retorting on them, to find contrast later in her stern, measured defense of Rome; Marcius finally brought to bay, fatally unchanged—here are many sorts of eloquence validly provided for. But there will be—and as legitimately—more likeness than difference in the matter of it, and between the speakers. For Menenius, Cominius and the Tribunes, Marcius and his mother, even the Volscians and Aufidius look—if not always from one standpoint—all towards the same horizon. There is the difference, truly, that less bitterness goes to battling against Volscian neighbors without the gates than against enemy kindred within. And this likeness lends to the temper of the verse a consistency which Marcius' own inevitable domination of it will but confirm, since there is little to be expressed in him that outranges the scope of the rest. And here again the close woven pattern of event and character, the internecine in the struggle, is an element of the tragedy.

There is nothing profound in Marcius, nor anything to set him inwardly apart from friend or foe, and all introspection is foreign to him. Of his two brief soliloquies, one is little more than an outburst of febrile ill-temper, a climax to his infatuate protest against donning the gown of humility and asking the citizens for their votes:

> Better it is to die, better to starve,
> Than crave the hire which first we do deserve.
> Why in this woolvish gown should I stand here,
> To beg of Hob and Dick, that does appear,
> Their needless vouches? . . .

—and the exceptional succession of six rhymed couplets with their jangling iteration goes to painting this. The second is detached comment, hardly more. He is in Antium, the revolution within him already accomplished.

> O world, thy slippery turns! . . .

If we hear of no doubts or misgivings or struggles of conscience it is because there will have been none. Plunged in misery,

> Longer to live most weary . . .

by a sudden "slippery turn" he has become—so he supposes—another man:

> My birth-place hate I, and my love's upon
> This enemy town.

It is as simple as that. Of the workings of a troubled mind he knows no more than does a child. He is frank and direct with mother, wife or friend, eloquent in anger. Of the inward Marcius we have passing glimpses only; in his thought for his one-time host in Corioles, for the widows his valor has left grieving there; in his respect for his mother, his chaste love for his wife; finally in the resigned realization of

> Not of a woman's tenderness to be,
> Requires nor child nor woman's face to see.

—its reflective cadence throwing it gently into relief against the stronger rhythm of the current speech.

## The Question of Act-Division

THE play's action falls dramatically into three main divisions. The first, after some preliminary excursions into the citizens' discontent, covers the Volscian war; the second begins with Marcius' triumphant return from it, develops the struggle around his consulship and finishes upon his banishment; the third runs from his surrender to Aufidius, through the threats and alarms of his return, the surrender to his mother and the catastrophe of the end. This, however, being among the plays first found in the Folio, is there submitted to the formal five-act division—which, lacking more than once any dramatic warrant, one doubts to be Shakespeare's. A tricky question to answer, this of act-division; since we do not very certainly know how, at performances—and with what consistency—the act-pause was used. As a ten-minute interval during which the audience could relax? As a more formal minute's breathing-space for the actors? The punctuating power of the act-division will differ greatly.

What dramatic value can there be in the Folio's division here that parts Act II from Act III? In the action itself there is continuity. In Marcius' own tones and in his friends' attitude towards him, their deference to him as "Lord Consul," his readiness for more war with the Volscians, one may perhaps distinguish a change of key; but nothing, one would say that needs an act-division—certainly not a long pause—for its emphasis. Again, a fresh dramatic chapter in the story certainly begins with Coriolanus' appearance at Antium, *in mean apparel, disguised and muffled*. Just before this comes the "bridge scene" between the Roman and Volscian spies; and, from a dramatic standpoint, the Folio could suitably either end its third act with this or begin its fourth. It does neither. And if the practical convenience of a Marcius who must doff his Consul's insignia to make himself all but unrecognizable in his mean apparel ought also to be considered—it is not. Nor does there seem to be any very patent dramatic reason for ending a fourth act where the Folio ends this, nor for beginning the fifth act with Menenius setting forth on his errand after refusing to.

We may feel certain, surely, that Shakespeare sought, first and last, to make his plays dramatically viable, although we may not be so certain as we begin to think we are of the effects made by his stage on his stagecraft. But when we can be fairly certain of this, it is good evidence that what offends against these effects is not from his hand.

# The Stage Directions

SOME of these are among the play's most notable features. Incidentally, their dramatic value apart, they stand among the items of evidence of a retirement to Stratford and the writing of the latest plays in a semi-detachment from the theater. Such evidence is, of course, inferential, no better than guesswork if you will. But *Coriolanus* at least speaks in this respect pretty plainly of a manuscript to be sent to London, and of a staging which the author did not expect to supervise himself.

The directions are always expert, devised by someone who has visualized the action very clearly. They may be such a mere memorandum as a prompter might write in, as where, in the passage covering the battle for Corioles, after the customary indicative

> *The fight is renewed. The Volsces retire into Corioles, and*
> *Marcius follows them to the gates.*

comes for Marcius the mandatory

> *Enter the gates.*

One builds nothing on that. But

> *Enter Cominius, as it were in retire, with soldiers.*

and later

> *Enter two Officers, to lay cushions, as it were, in the Capitol.*

—these "as it weres" are, so to say, "advisory"; the actors must devise their expression for themselves. On the other hand, action of dramatic importance may be underlined, though the spoken text indicate it clearly enough:

> *Enter Coriolanus, in a gown of humility . . .*

and the next words spoken are

> Here he comes, and in the gown of humility. . . .

And later—though nothing will be plainer than the sight itself—

> *Enter Coriolanus, in mean apparel, disguised and muffled.*

Here is the author, stressing these effects upon the actors, for his own satisfaction, to make sure they miss none of them; for his own great satisfaction, one feels, when it comes to

> *Draw both the Conspirators and kils Martius, who falles,*
> *Auffidius stands on him.*

And

> *Enter Menenius to the Watch or Guard.*

"*Watch or Guard*"; whichever you please, it comes to the same thing.

But the direction to be valued most of all is that given to the actor of Marcius himself. Before he yields to Volumnia he

> *Holds her by the hand, silent.*

—for an appreciable moment, it must be. Had Shakespeare had his actors at hand to direct should we now ever have had that?

Did a foolishly rash Macbeth go speeding on after the sledge-hammer blow of

> The Queen, my lord, is dead.

Not if Shakespeare was there to stop him!

## Corry-ols, Corry-o-les, or Corī-o-les; Corry-o-lanus or Corī-o-lanus?

It is related of John Philip Kemble that once, when making at the end of a performance the customary announcement of the next, he told the house that the company would present Shakespeare's play of Corry-o-lanus in which he himself would undertake the part of Corī-o-lanus.[64] Such disputes would occasionally enliven the already livelier theater of those days, resembling as it could—the "Pit" of it—rather an unruly club than a mere shop in which plays are so tamely bought and sold. And while, despite three centuries of searching out—and willfully creating!—Shakespearean problems, there remain more than enough to be solved, few, whether of greater or less import, offer us such a free choice as does this. Nor is it of such little dramatic import as the pronunciation of a word will commonly be. It proclaims the hero's glory; its refusal to him is the final insult which he will not brook; at a dozen moments it is made the keynote of eloquence and emotion. The cadence of the word, and its music; those, therefore, are, dramatically, the two important things about it. Whatever Shakespeare's intention, we may be certain that he meant it to sound well.

It is not first met with precisely in that form, but coming from a Volscian Senator in his jaunty

> Let us alone to guard Cor-ī-oles. . . .

which is as simple a decasyllable as the play contains. But when, two scenes later, a messenger enters with his news, this is that

> The citizens of Corry-ols have issued,
> And given to Lartius and to Marcius battle. . . .

---

[64] I have the story from that able, and now so deeply regretted, theatrical historian Harold Child.

and the minor actor who did anything but stress the "Corry . . ." might count, surely, upon sharp correction. Yet only twenty-three lines later Marcius will be all but bound to say that Titus Lartius is

> Holding Co-ri-o-les in the name of Rome . . .

—and would possibly not be so amenable to correction. And a little later he tells Aufidius,

> Within these three hours, Tullus,
> Alone I fought in your Co-ri-o-les walls. . . .

And what other than the longest of long ī's can that Corioles contain?

But here, of course, are sources only of the "Coriolanus" of our question; and this, when it first appears a scene later, still is so much a proclamation (with an exulting echo) that it can be counted out of the verse and its demands altogether. One can only say that as it is surrounded by "Corioles" (one before and two after), with their long ī's indubitable, "Corīolanus" would seem to be the most instinctive derivative.

It comes again in the verse of a proclamation; and the Herald may have it either way he will—or both.

> Know, Rome, that all alone Marcius did fight
> Within Corioles gates, where he hath won . . .

(there is the long ī undoubtedly)

> With fame, a name to Caius Marcius: these
> In honour follows Corry-o-lanus.

with, to conclude, either a

> Welcome to Rome, renownèd Corry-o-lanus!

or a

> Welcome to Rome, renowned Cor-ī-olanus!

which you choose; Volumnia also having her choice between a poor line in

> What is it? Corry-o-lanus must I call thee?

and a better one in

> What is't? Cor-ī-olanus must I call thee?

—being sure, in rehearsal at any rate, of loud ironic protests from the rest of the company when, with a wink, she poses the problem!

Thereafter, however, and on all hands, the pronunciation "Corry-o-lanus" slides more easily into the verse, though never stimulating it. Sicinius can even squeeze a certain mockery into the tunelessness of

> Your Corry-olanus is not much missed
> But with his friends. . . .

Again, Volumnia will do the better with

> To his surname Cor-ī-olanus longs more pride
> Than pity to our prayers.

though the verse does not force it on her, and fits the word ill at best. But "Cor-ī-o-les," a minute later, it must be.

With the play's closing moments we are nearing the name's most pointedly dramatic use. Aufidius'

> Ay, Marcius, Caius Marcius. Dost thou think
> I'll grace thee with that robbery, thy stolen name
> Coriolanus in Corioles?

"Corry-o-lanus in Corry-ols" or "Corry-o-les" it certainly cannot be; "Corry-o-lanus in Cor-i-o-les" it just may be. But how much finer "Cor-ī-olanus in Cor-ī-o-les"! And what Marcius will hesitate an instant over

> "Boy"! false hound!
> If you have writ your annals true, 'tis there,
> That, like an eagle in a dove-cote, I
> Fluttered your Volscians in Cor-ī-o-les. . . .

"Corry-o-lanus," then, it would seem has the majority of voices. But let there never be one for "Corry-ols" or "Corry-o-les"!

One is tempted towards what is, doubtless, an indefensible heresy. Were the Elizabethans as inconsistent in the pronouncing of some uncommon words as in the spelling of them? Was it as possible for an actor to say "Corry-o-lanus" at one moment and "Cor-ī-olanus" at another—whichever suited the verse the better —with none of the hearers finding the change objectionable as it would be for a dramatist to sign himself "Shakespeare" at one moment and "Shaxpeer" the next? It would need, of course, a braver man than the present writer to plead this.